HOSTING THE HOLY SPIRIT

CHÉ AHN

General Editor

Renew
FROM REGAL

A Division of Gospel Light
Ventura, California, U.S.A.

Published by Renew Books
A Division of Gospel Light
Ventura, California, U.S.A.
Printed in the U.S.A.

Renew Books is a ministry of Gospel Light, an evangelical Christian publisher dedicated to serving the local church. We believe God's vision for Gospel Light is to provide church leaders with biblical, user-friendly materials that will help them evangelize, disciple and minister to children, youth and families.

It is our prayer that this Renew book will help you discover biblical truth for your own life and help you meet the needs of others. May God richly bless you.

For a free catalog of resources from Renew Books/Gospel Light, please call your Christian supplier or contact us at 1-800-4-GOSPEL or www.regalbooks.com.

Cover and Interior Design by Robert Williams
Edited by David Webb

Library of Congress Cataloging-in-Publication Data
Hosting the Holy Spirit / Ché Ahn, general editor.
        p. cm.
      ISBN 0-8307-2584-9
      1. Holy Spirit.   2. Spiritual Life—Christianity.   I. Ahn, Ché, 1956–

    BT121.2 .H67   2000
    269—dc21   00-059248

1 2 3 4 5 6 7 8 9 10 11 12 13 14 15 / 09 08 07 06 05 04 03 02 01 00

Rights for publishing this book in other languages are contracted by Gospel Literature International (GLINT). GLINT also provides technical help for the adaptation, translation and publishing of Bible study resources and books in scores of languages worldwide. For further information, write to GLINT, P.O. Box 4060, Ontario, CA 91761-1003, U.S.A. You may also send e-mail to Glintint@aol.com, or visit the GLINT website at www.glint.org.

CONTENTS

CROSSROADS

We are standing at a crossroads in this hour of renewal. Even as the Church is experiencing many glorious acts of the Holy Spirit, we have before us a very important decision to make.

How grateful we are to enjoy the presence of God in our midst! How marvelous is the goodness of God to embrace us with joy, tears and even shaking, all the while moving us to change through repentance and intimacy with Him! How precious is the tangible love of God that is bringing hearts to salvation!

Yet the question we must ask—and the decision we must make—is this: Are we living in a way that will invite this visitation of the Holy Spirit to remain and flourish? It is one thing to play host to the Spirit for a season, as though welcoming a guest lecturer, however illustrious; it is quite another to make a place in the life of your church for the Spirit of the King of glory to dwell. Will we make room for a *habitation* of the Holy Spirit and not just a *visitation*?

The answer to this question is the motivation for this book. Of course we earnestly desire to see the Holy Spirit remain in our midst and increase His presence all across the globe. Contributing authors to this work are all leaders who have found different places of favor before the Lord through His grace to cause the Holy Spirit to remain and grow.

Although this is not an exhaustive work on what draws the precious person of the Holy Spirit to abide with us, we should cherish every insight into how we might live a life that pleases Him and will further cause Him to dwell wonderfully among us, transforming hearts and lives until the Lord's return.

AN HONORED GUEST

Have you ever wondered why some churches are more blessed than others? Or why the presence of God can be more readily felt and enjoyed in these places? I believe these blessed churches have learned well how to host the Holy Spirit. The Spirit of God is welcomed, appreciated and honored in these churches and is thus delighted to abide there.

Think of a favorite place you like to go, such as a restaurant or the home of a friend or relative. Most likely it is one of your favorite places because there you are treated like someone special. I love to visit my parents' home because they lavish me with love and hospitality.

Conversely, we have all visited establishments where the service was poor or homes where we felt unwelcome. Perhaps we were invited or served only out of obligation rather than genuine love or desire. I believe the Third Person of the Godhead perceives this kind of acceptance or rejection in a similar fashion.

I once heard the story of a black man who tried to attend a white church shortly after the Civil War. He was unceremoniously asked to leave the service. As he was walking down the road, Jesus walked up beside him and inquired what was wrong. The man replied that he tried to visit this white churchs, but they had rejected him. Jesus comforted the man, saying, "Don't feel bad. They rejected Me, too."

How many times do we reject the Holy Spirit, shutting Him out of our churches or homes without knowing it? How often do we grieve Him, intentionally or unintentionally?

This book looks at ways you can best host the Holy Spirit—both in your own personal life and in the life of your church. For where the Holy Spirit is welcomed, He brings His favor and His blessing. Recall when the Ark of the Covenant was placed in the home of Obed-Edom:

> The ark of the LORD remained in the house of Obed-Edom the Gittite for three months, and the LORD blessed him and his entire household. Now King David was told, "The LORD has blessed the household of Obed-Edom and everything he has, because of the ark of God." So David went down and brought up the ark of God from the house of Obed-Edom to the City of David with rejoicing (2 Sam. 6:11,12, *NIV*).

The ark is where the presence of the Holy Spirit dwelled. Where God's presence remains, the wonderful favor and blessing of God always come. Whether this favor results in full-blown revival or simply the sweet manifestation of His presence, there can be no greater privilege and delight.

Let us endeavor to host the Holy Spirit with all that is within us!

DR. CHÉ AHN
Pastor, Harvest Rock Church
Pasadena, California

VALUING THE ANOINTING

by John Arnott

John Arnott is senior pastor of Toronto Airport Christian Fellowship in Toronto, Ontario, Canada. For more than seven years, his church has experienced a sustained outpouring of the Holy Spirit known around the world as the Father's Blessing, or the Toronto Blessing. An incredible presence of God envelops those who attend and those who visit. As the Holy Spirit descends upon each service, many can be found joyously laughing, crying in repentance, experiencing spontaneous healing, being emotionally set free or physically delivered, or lying prostrate on the floor, soaking in the presence of God and resting under the power of the Spirit. Since January 1994, more than two million people have come to Toronto to experience the blessing, and many have taken this transferable love back to their home churches and cities around the world. John Arnott is a dear friend who has had a profound impact upon our church in Pasadena. It is an honor to have him contribute the first chapter of this book.

Because of God's wonderful visitation upon our church in Toronto, I have discovered an important truth of the Kingdom: Only the anointing and presence of the Holy Spirit—and nothing else—will cause ordinary people like you and me to enter into a place of phenomenal Kingdom success.

You can have the best organized prayer groups, the best cell-group strategy, the best multimedia presentation, the best choir, the best preaching, the best teaching—the best of everything, and with all these, you may reach a few people. But if you are working without the anointing of the Holy Spirit, without the presence of God upon you, you are *not* going to rock *cities*. You are *not* going to change *nations*. You will *not* be able to walk in *all God has for you*. The Holy Spirit is the key to reaching the world.

Before this outpouring in our midst, my wife, Carol, and I had seen brief displays of what God was willing to do among His people. We had experienced some moves of the Holy Spirit, but we had never seen anything of this magnitude sustained for long. Now, more than seven years since the beginning of the visitation at Toronto Airport Christian Fellowship, we find that although we are eternally grateful for this move of God in our lives, we are still hungry for more.

Even as we enjoy all that God has given us, I sometimes wonder why this blessing hasn't spread like holy wildfire around the world. Why haven't millions more people received the blessing and come into the Kingdom because they witnessed God's tangible goodness and love? I think, *Lord, what's taking so long?* while another part of me already knows the answer. The delay has to do with our own readiness in terms of how we treat the Holy Spirit when He drops by for a visit. Do we really *value* the presence of God? Do we really value His anointing?

Unless we treasure God's presence when He comes and make it a point to keep watch over our hearts, we can become so accustomed to the anointing that we begin to treat the Spirit like part of the furnishings and décor. We begin to think, *Well, this is just the Holy Spirit here again. Yes, people do funny things. They fall down, they get noisy, they run around. That's just what happens when the Holy Spirit is around.* We can become distracted by all the activity to the point that we begin to overlook the truly miraculous things that are happening as the Holy Spirit moves among us. We can start to take the Spirit of God for granted and fail to value this amazing, precious gift that God has given us.

I've told my own church that I'm not the pastor of our congregation. The Holy Spirit is the pastor of our church, and whatever He wants to do, that's what we will do, to the best of our ability. When I pause to consider where our church would be without His presence, I begin to realize just how much He has really changed us through this visitation. I've talked with many people, members and guests, about their experiences with this move of God; most have told me their lives have been radically altered in the last few years. I know mine has been. I would probably still be content to pastor a church of five or six hundred people, blissfully ignorant of all that is possible with the anointing and presence of God.

A JADED PEOPLE

Every time you see the Holy Spirit come upon someone or you encounter His presence through the anointing, something inside you should explode with rejoicing! I pray you would see that this is more than just an outward sign—that you would recognize the manifest presence of the Lord God at work. Know that He is bringing forth the joy of the Lord. He is dancing on the enemy's head, treading on serpents and scorpions and the enemies of our soul. He is healing heart wounds and bringing physical and emotional release. What an incredible blessing!

It's a wonderful, joyful thing to have God showing up in your meetings night after night after night. But human nature being what it is, especially in our culture, we must force ourselves to stop and focus on what is really going on. As a society, we've become a people who cannot be shocked—or thrilled. By the time our youth reach the age of 18, they've seen 18,000 murders on television. We've learned to block out all kinds of pandemonium. Then God Himself comes to church and works wonders in our midst. We passively acknowledge His presence and think, *Well, I guess that's good.*

We need to seriously take hold of the fact that before our very eyes, God is doing what He promised thousands of years ago: He's pouring out His Spirit on *all* flesh! He is taking up residence among His people! Many prophets and righteous men and kings have desired to see what we see, to hear what we hear. We must learn to value His presence among us.

One way we value the anointing among us is to allow God's character and nature to be built in us so that we may use the anointing properly. Then we will touch the world for His glory and not our own. God wants to place His anointing on men and women of integrity who can carry the fire and the presence of the living God to a desperate, broken and needy world. How effective these men and women are will depend on their response to God.

The lives of two men of the Old Testament dramatically illustrate the differences in whether or not we choose to value the anointing. One of these men is the mighty Samson; the other is the prophet Elisha.

SAMSON FAILED TO VALUE THE ANOINTING

The time is about 1200 B.C. The place is the land of Canaan. The nation of Israel is in trouble, for the Lord has delivered His people into the hands of their enemies the Philistines for a period of 40 years. One day the angel of the Lord appears to the wife of Manoah of Zorah. This woman is barren and childless, but the angel announces God's marvelous plan to give her a son who will be instrumental in the deliverance of Israel. She will give birth to Samson.

According to the angel's instructions, Samson's parents are never to take him to the local barber for a trim. He is to be set apart for the things of God, for he is destined to become a mighty, anointed man of war who will lead the children of Israel to freedom.

And, of course, he will possess incredible strength. One day when he is a young man, Samson's enemies will set a trap for him in Gaza (see Judg. 16:1-3). Samson will get wise to the plot and walk off with the city gates, posts and all, and carry them to the top of a nearby hill. (The people of Gaza no doubt were confounded and perplexed—not unlike the world's response to what is happening in the Church today. You see, the world has no way to comprehend or deal with the anointing of God. They don't know what to do with that kind of strength!)

Samson is born, and as he grows, the Lord blesses him and the Spirit of the Lord begins to "stir him" (Judg. 13:25). It is a glorious beginning for Samson, growing up with the anointing of God upon him from his earliest memories.

So what does Samson do with the anointing when the time comes to make his first real-life choices? He goes down to Timnah and falls in love with a young Philistine woman! When he returns home, he *demands* that his parents get the woman to be his wife. With wisdom and concern, his father and mother ask if there is not an acceptable woman among their own people. "Must you go to the uncircumcised Philistines to get a wife?" they ask (Judg. 14:3, *NIV*).

(This is a disturbing dynamic that is all too familiar, yet one that I still find mysterious after many years in ministry. It is puzzling how a person can have such great anointing on the one hand and an appetite for carnality on the other.)

Later, as Samson is traveling to visit his girl in Timnah, a young lion comes roaring toward him. The Spirit of the Lord comes upon Samson in power, and he tears the lion apart with his bare hands. Now, if you were on your way to marry an ungodly woman, and a lion came out of the bush, you might stop to wonder, *Is there the slightest possibility this could be a sign?* But Samson only presses on toward what *he* wants.

This is the first of several instances in which Samson will use the anointing of God for his own protection or personal gain. During his ministry as judge over the Israelites, Samson will use the anointing to

- Compose a riddle that will vex his enemies and demonstrate his own cleverness (see Judg. 14:14)
- Pay off a gambling debt (see Judg. 14:19)
- Take his revenge by catching 300 foxes, tying torches to their tails and setting fire to the Philistines' fields and vineyards (see Judg. 15:4,5)
- Escape capture by breaking his bonds and slaying a thousand Philistines with the jawbone of a donkey (see Judg. 15:14,15)

If you're like me, right about now you're thinking, *Wait a minute, I don't get this. An angel comes to Samson's mother and calls him into life to be a warrior, a man of integrity. Instead he uses the anointing to serve his own selfish interests! Doesn't he know what an incredible gift he's been given? Doesn't he understand what he's supposed to do with it?*

The Enemy Will Wear You Down

Once they have seen enough of Samson, the lords of the Philistines go to his new girlfriend, Delilah, and they each offer to pay her 1100 pieces of silver if she can lure Samson into revealing the secret of his great strength so that they might overpower him and be rid of him once and for all.

The painful plot is set into motion. When Delilah coyly asks Samson the source of his great strength, he teases her with different false replies. First, he tells her that if she ties him up with seven fresh bow strings, he will be as weak as any other man. Then he sins with her all night long. In the night, she ties him up with seven fresh bow strings and shouts, "Samson, the Philistines are upon you!" To her chagrin, he gets up, breaks the cords from his wrists and gets away.

Delilah pressures him again, saying he has made a fool of her. Samson tells her to tie him securely with new ropes that have never been used and he will become as weak as other men. More sin, more falling asleep, more tying him up. Again she declares, "Samson, the Philistines are upon you." Again, he gets up and breaks the new ropes.

You have to wonder what kind of a mind would allow this to continue. Every time Samson tells her his supposed secret, Delilah tests it. He is foolishly playing around, flirting with the enemy, who is all the while pressing in on him, wearing him down and moving in for the kill. Satan knows this is a very dangerous person who is powerfully called and anointed of God; but he also knows that Samson is susceptible because of his carnal side. Samson desires to do things his way and in his time and thus has given the enemy an opportunity to take him down.

"Tired to death" of her nagging, Samson tells Delilah the truth about his strength: "If my head were shaved, my strength would leave me, and I would become as weak as any other man" (Judg.

16:16,17, *NIV*). Sure enough, she calls in her stylist to give Samson a new look while he sleeps. When Delilah calls out, "Samson, the Philistines are upon you," he wakes up and figures he will escape as before. What he doesn't know is that the Lord has left him.

This is a tragic story. The Philistines seize Samson, gouge out his eyes and set him to grinding in their prison. This pretty much ends the ministry of a man whom God had planned to use mightily to bring great release to a nation.

Samson Had His Own Agenda

Samson had several problems that led to his failure, any of which each and every one of us can fall victim to. But perhaps the most dangerous was that Samson became used to the anointing. I frequently pray, *Please, Father, somehow, some way, don't let me get used to this. You've been pouring out Your Spirit on us all these weeks and months and years, and You come here every night. There are times when we haven't had time to pray—or haven't taken time—and still You come. When we are unfaithful, You are faithful still. God, please help us. Don't ever let us take this anointing for granted!*

We must watch over our hearts and make sure we never get "ho-hum" about the fact that the Spirit of God has visited us and is continuing to visit us. The destiny of your city is quite possibly intertwined with your faithfulness! The destiny of the nation of Israel was intertwined with the anointing of Samson, and he failed miserably because he had his own agenda. He missed what God wanted to do and found himself blind, bound and stumbling around, grinding at the mill. What a horrible way to end up.

It's possible that many ministries now being visited by the Holy Spirit will meet the same fate and, in fact, already have. In just the last few years, Carol and I have met with several ministries and pastors who believed that somehow "this Toronto thing," this

"Holy Spirit thing," could be useful to them or help their church-es grow. Some of these leaders wanted the anointing but chose not to deal with issues of secret sin in their own hearts. There will one day come a warning and a dealing of the Lord over these issues and then all of a sudden—boom!—it will all be over. When the enemy comes and puts out your eyes, it is a terrible, terrible thing.

Samson had a lust problem, but his weakness for Philistine women was not his greatest challenge. His problem was that he failed to value his calling, to prize the anointing that God had placed in his life. He was no ordinary person; some-thing wonderful had come upon him! But did he ever stop to ask, *Why me?* He shared the secret of his strength with the enemy, but did he ever really tell anyone of the wondrous power of God? Did he ever use his gift to bene-fit anyone other than himself?

GOD, PLEASE HELP US! DON'T EVER LET US TAKE YOUR ANOINTING FOR GRANTED.

When you partake of the wonder-ful anointing of renewal, something very precious comes upon you. There is a person of the Holy Spirit whom you cannot see but who surrounds you. You can put your hands into that Presence. You can stick your feet into that Presence. You can breathe that Presence, right down to your innermost being. It is God, the Holy Spirit, and He has come to anoint you, to equip you and to cause you to become a super-natural person in the hands of God who will bring deliverance to your people and your nation.

Yet the Bible is full of stories about people who had an anoint-ing and blew it. Consider Judas. How could you spend three years with Jesus and then turn him over to the enemy for a few silver coins? You would never meet such a lovely person as Jesus. But money is funny stuff. It's what motivated Delilah, and it's what captured Judas. I ask you: What would you take in exchange for the anointing? What would the devil have to offer you to get you to compromise?

Let's look at another man's response to the anointing.

ELISHA VALUED THE ANOINTING

Unlike Samson, Elisha was raised a farm boy with nothing in his birth or upbringing to indicate that he was to become a prophet and a mighty man of God. As far as I can tell, all he had was a strong desire to serve and a deep love for the anointing—qualities he demonstrated after Elijah, the great prophet of Israel, recruited Elisha to leave the farm and accompany him for the remainder of his ministry.

Sometime later, the day comes when a revelation of the Spirit informs the prophets of God that Elijah is going to be taken up into heaven. That same day, the prophet Elijah and his protégé Elisha are on their way from Gilgal when Elijah tells his charge, "Stay here; the LORD has sent me to Bethel." But Elisha knows what is coming; and he refuses, saying, "As surely as the LORD lives and as you live, I will not leave you" (2 Kings 2:2, *NIV*).

So together they go on to Bethel, where the prophets of Bethel (who are perhaps jealous of the great Elijah and his destiny) confront Elisha: "Do you not know that the LORD is going to take your master from you today?" Young Elisha will not be deterred. He pushes through public opinion and answers with firm resolve, "Listen, this is none of your business. Don't speak of it. Just stay out of it" (see v. 3). Elisha loves the anointing and that drives him onward.

The scenario is repeated as the Lord then sends Elijah to Jericho (see v. 4) and later to the Jordan (see v. 6). Elisha refuses to leave his master, knowing that the Lord is going to take the great prophet from him that very day. Meanwhile, 50 men of the company of the prophets follow them at a distance, waiting to see what will happen.

When they arrive at the Jordan River, Elijah takes his cloak, rolls it up and strikes the water with it. The water divides to the right and the left, and the two men cross to the other side on dry ground. When they have crossed, Elijah says to Elisha, "Tell me what I can do for you before I am taken from you."

"Let me inherit a double portion of your spirit," Elisha replies (v. 9).

"You've asked a difficult thing," Elijah says, scratching his beard. "If you see me when I am taken from you, what you ask will be yours. Otherwise, it will not" (see v. 10).

So they continue walking and talking together when, suddenly, a chariot of fire drawn by horses of fire appears between them. Elijah climbs aboard and departs for heaven in a whirlwind, and Elisha sees him no more.

Then Elisha notices his master's cloak lying on the ground nearby. He picks up the cloak and goes back and stands on the bank of the Jordan. He wants to see if the cloak will work for him, if he indeed has received the anointing. He takes the cloak and strikes the water with it, saying, "Where now is the LORD, the God of Elijah?" Pretty cheeky. But when he strikes the water, it once again divides to the right and the left, and Elisha crosses over. When the company of prophets who were watching see that the spirit of Elijah is resting on Elisha, they rush to meet him and bow to the ground before him (see 2 Kings 2:13-15).

I love that story.

Elisha Wanted More

When Elijah tested his protégé—"You stay here"—Elisha said, "Nothing doing. Something big is going down, and today of all days I am not leaving your side." This happened three times, which leads me to ask a question: How badly do *you* want *more*? You see, it's going to take more of the anointing for us to see the hidden places of our hearts changed, our families saved and our cities rocked for God.

If you are experiencing renewal in your life and church, think back to where you used to be before He touched you. Now imagine where you might be if the Lord *multiplied* the anointing that's on you 10 times over—or 100! Elisha wanted *more*, and he would not leave Elijah's side. He passed the test and got the double portion he was after.

In our lives we face the same kind of tests. Your friends or your neighbors or your mother or your relatives don't like this move of God you're experiencing, and they can make it hard for you. Some of them may even think you've flipped out! I'm sure Elisha's family wondered about him sometimes. The testing came. Contemporaries in the ministry were telling him to back off, to get out of the way, because something big was happening with Elijah. But Elisha just pressed into God all the more, and he stuck to Elijah like glue.

I try to picture myself in Elisha's place that day at the river. He loves the anointing. He's seen God do so many wonderful things. He's going to miss Elijah, a great man of God. What do you ask for at a time like that? If I were having a really good day, I might boldly say, "Elijah, I want what you have. The anointing that is on you—I want that." But Elisha dared to ask for more.

Elisha Received a New Mantle

Elisha had already proven his character and his love for the anointing. So when he asked Elijah for a double portion of his anointing, the prophet didn't rebuke him, although he acknowledged that Elisha had asked a very hard thing. The answer depended upon Elisha's ability to see Elijah caught up to heaven. Imagine walking along with a prophet of God one minute, and the next minute he's gone! But Elisha did see. A veil was pulled back and Elisha saw into the spirit realm as angelic beings arrived on the scene and Elijah hitched a ride to the sky in a whirlwind of glory.

When Elisha saw the mantle, the cloak of Elijah, floating down from the sky, he probably couldn't wait to try it out. The first thing Elisha did was to throw his own anointing away. He pulled off his own cloak and tore it in two. He didn't need it anymore. He had Elijah's mantle now—not just the mantle Elijah had used on earth, but now, after this divine visitation, a mantle with a touch of heaven on it. The anointing had been doubled! Elisha took the mantle, went out and did twice as many miracles as Elijah had done. Similar anointing, twice as many miracles. This man valued the anointing.

Undoubtedly, Elisha had seen his mentor raise the dead. Hanging out with Elijah, he had indeed witnessed many miracles as chronicled in the Scriptures. *But he never got used to it.* Somehow, Elisha had never come to the place where he thought of the anointing of God as "old hat," no big deal. Elisha instead watched over his own heart and determined to treasure the anointing, to value it. He wanted more.

THE SPIRIT REMAINS WHERE THERE IS LOVE FOR THE ANOINTING

People often ask me why the visitation of the Holy Spirit remains in some places and lifts from others after a short time. I don't know that I have the full answer. Perhaps, in the wisdom of God, some places were only meant to have a two- or three-week visitation. But one thing I have noticed: The Spirit remains where there is a love for the anointing.

Not unlike most people, the Holy Spirit knows when He is welcome in a place. When He is welcome, He keeps coming back. When He is treated with disrespect or if He becomes an embarrassment to the church, He just stops coming. He knows when He is not wanted. We need to guard our hearts regarding what we think of Him!

A couple of years ago, my wife and I visited a church in New Zealand. The place was packed. Everyone had come to see if this move of God in Toronto was really as weird as they had heard. A lot of pastors were there, and I was hoping we could convince them that what we had been experiencing at our church was really of God. That night, we "lost" three worship leaders. One fell under the anointing while singing and was immediately "out" on the floor. So we sent another man up to lead worship. He got about halfway through the next song and then, BOOM! he was out, too. The same thing happened to the next one. We figured that was the end of our worship time, so the pastor got up and tried to say something. BOOM! His assistant got up and tried to say something. BOOM! Both were on the floor.

I was about the only scheduled speaker still on his feet, and I'm standing there wondering, *What is everybody thinking right about now? Lord, what are You doing?* The Holy Spirit spoke to me then and said, "Because you are honoring Me, I am honoring you with My presence."

Wow! I told the Lord honestly that I had come very close to being offended by what He was doing in that place. I confessed that I had been embarrassed—almost to the point of thinking, *I don't want this stuff.* I had failed to value the incredible treasure that was being poured out on that meeting. I made a promise to God that night never again to be embarrassed by His anointing.

You see, God didn't really care whether a few theologians were offended or a few Pharisees didn't like what they were seeing at that meeting. Instead, He cared that teenagers were being touched and set free and that children were seeing for the first time a demonstration of the power of the Spirit of God. He cared about hungry pastors and leaders whose hearts were being moved and who were falling in love with Jesus all over again.

I've interviewed hundreds of people in the aftermath of just that kind of meeting. I'll say something like, "I can see you really were impacted by something tonight. What was it?" Most of them will tell me, "Oh, I'm just so in love with Jesus. It was so real and powerful. Something has changed."

I will never again be embarrassed by what the Spirit does. I just need to know it's Him. As long as I know that what I am seeing is of Him, I don't need to be able to understand or explain it.

DO YOU WANT MORE?

Consider what it means to you to have the anointing of God present in your life and in your church. Do you truly appreciate what it means for the presence of God to inhabit your home or church for an extended visitation?

Much of North America has already said "No thanks" to His anointing. Little do they know that the Lord is testing hearts. He is looking for Elishas who will persevere through the difficult times, enduring the ridicule of men while continuing to love and seek after His face. When the opportunity comes, nothing will stop those who endure from pressing into God for a double portion.

Recently, Carol and I read the story of the priest Eli and his wicked sons in 1 Samuel 2—4. They had become so careless that they didn't even realize that the Spirit of the Lord wasn't with them anymore. The Bible says that in those days there were hardly any visions (see 1 Sam. 3:1), almost no outpouring of the Holy Spirit, and the judgment of God soon came upon Israel. The sons of Eli died in battle, and the Ark of the Covenant was captured. Soon after this calamity, Eli's daughter-in-law died in childbirth. Before she breathed her last, she named her son Ichabod, saying, "The glory has departed" (1 Sam. 4:21). The whole country was without hope. The presence of God had been taken from them because they did not value that rich treasure.

Let us stop moment by moment, day by day, and appreciate the immense treasure God has deposited in our earthen vessels. Let us never use the anointing to bail ourselves out, to cover our sins and mistakes as Samson did. Rather let us use the anointing to build the kingdom of God. May we remember what the anointing is for: "The Spirit of the Sovereign LORD is on me, because the LORD has anointed me to preach good news to the poor. He has sent me to bind up the brokenhearted, to proclaim freedom for the captives and release from darkness for the prisoners, to proclaim the year of the LORD's favor" (Isa. 61:1,2, *NIV*).

Holy Spirit, come and anoint us now. Build a foundation within us where our character is like the character of Jesus, and our giftedness is like His giftedness. Father, we want a double portion. Lord, we want to see our lives and our cities rocked by the power and the glory of God, the Holy Spirit. Father, call us now to press in like Elisha did. Lord, we love Your anointing, we value it, and we have the audacity to ask You for more. Take the Samson out of us, Lord, and make us like Elisha. Give us the double portion, we pray! Thank You, Lord! More!

BUILDING A MERCY SEAT

by Tommy Tenney

The best-selling author of The God Chasers *and* God's Dream Team,
*Tommy Tenney is a man with a passion for the presence of the Holy Spirit.
For more than three years, Tommy was instrumental in leading weekly revival
services at Rock City Church in Baltimore, Maryland. He has experienced the
miraculous, but more importantly he knows the value of intimacy with and
humility before the Lord. A personal friend and a mentor,
Tommy is a man who chases hard after God.*

People often ask why the Holy Spirit comes to a certain place or church—and why He remains there.

Many churches enjoy what some would call a *visitation* of the Holy Spirit, where there is a fresh outpouring and sense of God's presence and love. Yet all too often that presence lifts after a short time. Most often we find in our services a visitation from the Holy Spirit—but not a *habitation*.

How can we move from having the Holy Spirit visit us to having Him abide with us? I believe it has to do with the condi-

tion of our hearts and our willingness to build Him a place of
worship where He desires to remain. True, this must be a work
of the Spirit of God; but through Scripture, God has given us a
blueprint. It is called the mercy seat.

Our flesh is uncomfortable with such a place, the place
where God "will meet with you" (Exod. 30:6). The opportunity
to build such a place often comes at a point in our services when
we have been worshiping and are attempting to enter into the
Holy Place, into the presence of God. Most of the time in this situation we don't do as we should. We begin to get nervous with
the silence, with the lack of our being able to control every
move—and with the uncertainty of what God might do if we
truly gave Him liberty. Our flesh and our minds cry out for
somebody to do or say something to fill the awkward silence. Yet
that is exactly what we don't need—*somebody **doing** something!*
People have been doing things for a long, long time in our
churches . . . with very little to show for it.

The truth of the matter is that we don't need somebody
to do something—we need some *One*. We need God Himself to
move, to take us past the limits of our understanding and our
need and come to dwell among us. However, we're often so busy
developing the structure and plans for our services that we do
not allow for His presence, for interruptions, even from the Most
High. And He *won't* interrupt us if He's not invited. Yet a true
work of grace will only happen in our services if we make room
for Him to intervene and do something. We simply cannot do it
ourselves.

If great sermons were going to reach the world, it would have
already been reached. If wonderful programs were going to do it,
it would have already been done. Certainly, there have been great
sermons and wonderful programs! Yet what we are asking for is
bigger than what any man or group of men can do. So why do we

insist on trying to do it? What we really need to do is create an environment for the Holy Spirit to come and be welcome, because what we really need is *Him*. If it's going to get done, He's going to have to do it.

We need to quit looking to man to accomplish what only God can. We need to stop coming to church and focusing all our attention on a favorite person or speaker. If someone tells me they are coming to hear me preach, I warn them that they may be sadly disappointed. We must not come to church to hear a man; we must set our minds on the idea that we are there to meet with God!

John the Baptist fought with the same celebrity mind-set we struggle with today. "I am not the Christ," he protested to the crowds gathered around him. "I baptize with water, but there stands One among you whom you do not know. It is He who, coming after me, is preferred before me, whose sandal strap I am not worthy to loose" (John 1:20,26,27). John knew he was but flesh—nothing special. He pointed to the One coming in real power, but that didn't prevent people from worshiping the sign-post instead of following its direction.

David understood the true purpose in a gathering of God's people. He described in the psalms how we could simply stand in the presence of the Lord and minister to Him. David knew we didn't have to hype and manipulate the people, attempting to make something happen:

> Behold, bless the LORD, all you servants of the LORD, who by night stand in the house of the LORD! Lift up your hands in the sanctuary, and bless the LORD (Ps. 134:1,2).

We spend most of our time calling on God to minister to us. We want to receive from Him. But what causes the greatest visitation of God is when the flow of ministry goes *from us to Him*. The greatest flow comes when God doesn't just reach His hand down to earth to touch us, *but He comes and is enthroned and inhabits our worship* (see Ps. 22:3).

There is a pattern to how this happens. We may not understand it all, but we can stand in His presence, invite Him and let Him direct the flow. Where two or three are gathered together in His name, the Lord is in the midst of them (see Matt. 18:20). The Bible doesn't say that He is beside them but, rather, that He is in their very midst. What an incredible promise!

So we know He will come, but how do we cause Him to remain?

NO PLACE TO SIT

I believe that we need to learn how to host the Holy Spirit, to make Him feel comfortable and desire to remain. Let me tell you a story that illustrates this point. I have a wonderful friend whose name I won't mention because I wouldn't want to embarrass him. He's an anointed minister who has sacrificed much in his life to birth the things of God. He's literally broken open one entire nation to the gospel, and now there are thousands of churches in that country as a result of his labors. Our friendship goes way back. He's probably 20 or more years my senior. He came to my wedding and has been a part of much of my life. We're very close.

This friend suffers from a genetic disorder that causes severe obesity. He's short and wide—the fact is, he's just about as wide as he is tall. We are close enough that over the years we have talked about his size and how it has affected his life. I've stood with him as he has struggled to overcome his weight. He has been vulnerable with me and has shown me the size of the heart inside the man. He's let me look past the noted speaker, the outward man, and let me see the pain. He is a great man of God. And because of his difficulty, he walks in utter humility.

He's told me of the indignities that he has endured on airlines and in restaurants and in public places. He has been cursed at, laughed at, made fun of and spitefully wronged. He's lived with his abnormal size since he was a boy, and he really, truly does battle with it to this day.

His size also hinders his social life—and for him, that is a painful consequence of his condition. He can spend time with his friends at certain restaurants and public places, but he cannot visit some of his friends in the intimacy of their homes. With tears streaming from his eyes he explained, "Tommy, I've broken my last chair. I'm not going to do it anymore." Many people don't have chairs sturdy enough to hold his weight. He cannot visit with his friends in their homes because they don't have anyplace for him to sit! "You would think they'd know by looking at me that *I can't just sit anywhere!*"

Sometimes, when he would go to his friends' homes to drop something off or pick something up, he would stand in the foyer and talk for a moment or two. Perhaps he wouldn't even take off his coat. While chatting, he would scan the room to see if there was any new furniture—something sufficient to support his weight. If he didn't see anything, then he'd excuse himself and leave, despite the sincere and loving pleas that he come inside and stay awhile.

God spoke to me through my friend's story. The Bible calls God's manifest presence His glory, or *chabod*. The word literally means weightiness. In our colloquial English, we would say that God *carries a lot of weight* around here. Is it possible that one of the reasons why God only seems to *visit* most of the time rather than remain is because we don't have the proper furniture to hold Him?

How many times has God stood at the door of our church services, scanning the room in hopes of finding a place solid enough for Him to sit? Sitting implies that someone is going to be there awhile. Having a place to sit may be the defining difference between visitation and habitation. Is it possible in all our preparations and all that we do that we have never prepared a place for the glory of God? Is it possible that God must stand just inside the door with coat and hat in hand because we are not really ready?

We know how to make man comfortable. Our churches have padded pews, air conditioning, greeters and child care. Our services follow a comfortable, predictable pattern. We wouldn't know what to do if the glory of God really showed up at one of our meetings! Yet we pray for visitations like the one that occurred on Azusa Street in the early 1900s. William Seymour, a humble, one-eyed black man, was the pastor who ushered in the presence of God on Azusa Street. Do you know how he spent a lot of his time during those revival services? It is recorded that he spent those services with his head in an apple crate. Hiding. Weeping.

Why? Because when God *really* shows up, there's not much else you can do. When God shows up, His consuming holiness confronts our comfortable hollowness.

We know how to accommodate man. The pattern for seats that men sit on comes from down here where we are. But when you want to build a seat for the tangible weightiness of God to sit on, you're building a whole different thing. The pattern for building a seat for God came from heaven—a long time ago.

BLUEPRINTS FOR THE MERCY SEAT

God spoke to Moses in Exodus 25 and told him to make a tabernacle according to the pattern He would show him. He told

Moses to make an ark out of acacia wood, two and a half cubits being the length of it, a cubit and a half the width of it, and a cubit and half its height. It was to be overlaid with pure gold, within and without, and topped with a crown of gold. Rings were to be cast of gold for the ark to be carried. The Testimony, which God would give to Moses, was to be placed inside this ark.

Then the Lord instructed Moses to make a mercy seat of pure gold. Two and a half cubits would be the length of the seat and a cubit and a half the width of it. Moses was to make two cherubim of gold—not just any gold, but beaten work, or hammered gold. These cherubim had to be beaten into position. On each end of the mercy seat would be a cherub, and they were to stretch forth their wings from on high and cover the mercy seat with their wings. Their faces were to look one to another and down toward the mercy seat.

The mercy seat was to be placed above the Ark of the Covenant and the testimony from the Lord placed inside the ark. Then the Lord gave an incredible promise:

> *And there I will meet with you,* and I will speak with you from above the mercy seat, from between the two cherubim which are on the ark of the Testimony, about everything which I will give you in commandment to the children of Israel (Exod. 25:22, emphasis added).

God then admonishes Moses, "And see to it that you make [all these things] according to the pattern which was shown you on the mountain" (Exod. 25:40). God had made an incredible promise of His continuing presence with the children of Israel if they would only follow His pattern and build a mercy seat and the ark according to His instruction.

The Lord described the cherubim that would adorn the

mercy seat, and carefully told how they would be placed in a position of worship over the mercy seat. They would be made of beaten
gold—carefully hammered into a position of worship.

How many of us are willing to be the building blocks for a
mercy seat? How many of us are pliable in every area of our lives—
allowing ourselves to be hammered into the position of gratitude
and adoration and living a life being purified into pure gold?
This is the kind of substance that is required to build a mercy seat
for God. These are the true materials required to build a seat that
can handle the weighty presence of God's glory.

It is not a light or casual relationship between the Craftsman
and the object (us) which forms beaten gold; the process requires
consistent, tedious, careful and loving labor. There is no other
way to build this seat.

This is the pattern of which God said, "If you will build it this
way, I will come and sit there." This is the pattern Moses received
on the mountain. It's a pattern he received in much the same way
as the apostle John did when God allowed him to see into heaven.
John saw the throne of God surrounded by many seraphim—an
entire holy host as far as the eye could see (see Rev. 5:11). Yet the
Lord made a promise to Moses that if *just two* would come and surround the mercy seat, He would come and sit right there!

There is such a power in the agreement of two. Can you
imagine being one of two completely yielded vessels beaten into
position as pure gold on the mercy seat? It would not only
change your marriage, your job and your family, but it could also
change your church, your city and the world.

WHEN GOD SHOWS UP

What happens when God comes and sits on that mercy seat? If
you build it right, I believe God comes and sits on it and looks

out on the people and instead of judging them, He has mercy on them. Love flows from His throne. People and nations are drawn to Him. Hearts are melted and changed. People are never again the same. God appears.

To understand this better, we need to consider what will happen when God comes and sits on the Judgment Seat. There is a day coming when, God has promised, He will come and sit in judgment over mankind. This will be a terrifying day. He will judge nations. He will judge hearts and the intentions of hearts. Eternal fates will be sealed. When God judges, a matter is forever settled and there is no appeal. This will be the great and terrible day of the Lord. But God has reserved the Day of Judgment for an appropriate time.

My concern is that too many churches and people are calling today for God to come and sit on the Judgment Seat. They are calling for God to judge their cities. I am not interested in calling for judgment on a city. It's very easy for us to build a judgment seat but, thankfully, that decision and timing belong to God. We need to cry out for His mercy, for His compassion, for His intervention, while there is still a day to repent. To build a mercy seat requires a whole different mind-set and lifestyle.

I want to be a part of a people who will build a place for God to come and dwell right in the midst of our cities. I want to see Him come and pour out streams of mercy to desperate people all over my town—in the streets, in the bars, in the secret places, upon the drug addicts, the prostitutes, the bitter and the sick.

It doesn't much matter to me where He comes first—which church, which city, which people builds the mercy seat first. I just want God to descend on our cities. I cry out to God to help us build some true, sturdy furniture of mercy so that instead of a visitation of God, we will have a habitation! We need God to come!

We've experienced some great visitations of God in recent years. We've even been worshiping when He stepped through the door. We've felt His heartbeat when He's said, "Maybe, just maybe, I'll be able to stay here this time." But has He been able to take off His hat or His coat and stay? How often does He continue to walk through our buildings, looking inconspicuously around, thinking, *I don't want to embarrass My people, but there is nowhere I can sit. There is nothing of great enough substance here, nothing that can bear My weightiness.*

Yes, He's walked among us. We have felt the stroke of His hand across our brows. People have been healed, and it's incredible. We have felt His love and how excited He was to see us. But too soon it was over. We said to ourselves, *That was great!* And we went back the next night for more. But what we are after now is not just visitation; it's a habitation. First, we have to build a mercy seat so visitation can become habitation.

Where He sits, His mercy radiates all over a city. Hardened hearts are changed. Drunks on skid row feel His presence. Bankers who cry themselves to sleep because their money is no security suddenly find new hope. Broken marriages are healed. Lonely teenagers find Jesus. Until that kind of mercy flows in a city, God has not really come to remain.

There has to be a point of origin. Every fountain has to have a fountainhead. Every well has to have to have a place of beginning, and every revival has to have a mercy seat where the grace of God comes and is dispensed to the city.

Each one of us can be a part of it. Each of us can become a fountainhead

WHEN GOD DWELLS AMONG US, HIS MERCY RADIATES ALL OVER A CITY.

by yielding our hearts, our lives. If each of us will personally build a mercy seat for God to sit on, we will collectively make a place for Him to come among us as a people and stay.

The pattern is very specific. It is not the same pattern which makes man comfortable, but it is not difficult to follow. God requires only purity, unity and humility.

REFINED AS GOLD

God prescribes that the mercy seat has to be made of pure gold; it must be a place of *absolute purity*. Absolute purity is far more difficult to achieve than partial purity. When you purify gold, you must raise the temperature to cause the impurities to rise. The first impurities to be removed are generally things like common dirt. The temperature continues to rise as zinc and other mineral impurities are skimmed off.

Do you know what the last impurity to be removed is before pure gold is obtained? The last thing removed in the gold-refining process is *silver*. Now, silver is a very precious metal, but it is not the *most* precious. When you're refining gold, silver is an impurity that must be removed!

God is very stringent about what He allows to remain in our lives as we go through the purification process. He is very specific about what is most precious—and what is pure. Sometimes in our rush to get out of the fire and away from the heat, we abandon the refining process too soon. What we are left with may be good, but it's not what is best.

God said the mercy seat was to be pure gold. Silver, as nice as it is, won't work for God to sit on; it is not substantial enough. A lot of churches, a lot of people and a lot of revivals have been short-circuited simply because they thought, *This is good, too. It's good enough*. But if you really want a divine habitation, you can't make a seat for God out of what is second best. You have to make the seat according to the pattern of the Lord, for that is where He has promised to sit.

UNITY: A COMMON FOCUS

You begin with a mercy seat of absolute purity. Then, God says, you take two worshipers. They are to face each other, with arms extended upward and toward each other over the mercy seat. God is making a point with this description of their position. You see, when the visitation of God comes, He moves in the midst of people. We usually have our chairs pointed toward the platform in a church, expecting God to move in the front. I can tell you from experience, however, that most movement happens in the midst of the people—right there in the seats.

God is always in the "between." That is why the Lord told the priests and the ministers to "weep between the porch and the altar" (Joel 2:17); He wanted their intercession to take place in the midst of where He appeared—where the people were. Typically, as modern churchgoers, we don't like in-between places. We like services with firm destinations. We want everything designed to exact specifications for *our* comfort. Yet God most often visits people in the in-between places.

If you build worshipers around the mercy seat according to God's blueprint, they are going to be facing each other; but they will be looking toward that mercy seat. Their eyes are going to be focused and fixed on God, with their wings hovering over His place of honor. They create a unique environment for His presence as they worship over this base of pure gold.

God wants to come into the midst of this kind of worship. He is searching, seeking, saying, "If I can find two worshipers who will not focus on each other or themselves, but have their eyes on the mercy seat . . . if they will use their 'wings' to create a canopy for My presence and My glory . . . that's all I need." God has to be covered by our worship, and the mercy seat built according to His design provides the environment for Him to come among us.

HUMILITY: BROKEN AND BEATEN

Remember, though, that these worshipers are not formed easily or cheaply. They are literally *beaten* into position. When one is being made, if a wing is stuck out too far, then with the force of a hammer it is shaped and put in its place until it is just right. And only purified gold can be easily beaten and molded into proper position.

Yet when life begins to beat at most of us, we find ourselves beaten *out* of position instead. We don't allow the forces that come against us to force us into that position of worship. God creates the atmosphere for you to run to Him with all the stresses and struggles of life. He really wants you to be in that position—a position of total dependence upon Him. If you truly want to be a worshiper, you've got to allow Him to beat you into that position. Embrace the brokenness and refining that comes from God. Be humble as He molds you and lovingly forces you into position. For He says, "If you will let me put you into position, I will come and be right there in your midst."

God is looking for a church, a group of people who will lift their hands, just like the pattern on the ark. If you want God to come and *remain*, you've got to build the right chair. You know what the chair looks like. The cherubim are in a worshiping position over the mercy seat, their arms surrendered in the air. They can and will worship over Him under any circumstances. They are beaten into place, purified.

I am sure God knows what a chair looks like. To your eyes and my eyes, this kind of sacrifice and lifestyle doesn't look like a seat. But to God's eyes, this is His La-Z-Boy! It is His perfect recliner, His place of comfort. Our worship creates a comfort zone for the Holy Spirit.

The reason why we have experienced visitation but not habitation is that we have not provided a place of comfort for Him to remain. If we will just embrace the fullness of what makes Him comfortable and create a place for Him right in the middle of His worshipers, He will come into our midst and let His mercy flow from this seat to the entire city. But when we allow stresses to get us out of place, when we stray from our place over that mercy seat of worship, God must simply say, "I'm sorry, but I'll wait until this mercy seat gets repaired before I come and sit."

WORSHIP NOW!

A restoration of the Tabernacle of David is coming—a restoration that will be caught, not just taught. With a depth of understanding not previously known, God's people will learn what worship is all about. This may seem like it borders on sacrilege, but I need to say it: *Worship is more important to God than preaching*. If we're not careful, we will value talking *about* Him above talking *to* Him. Preaching is meant to get us into the position to be worshipers; instead we tend to worship our preaching.

God must be our focus. When we come together in purity, unity and humility, God will come right into our midst. The Bible says that God is enthroned by the praises of His people (see Ps. 22:3). If two of us will stand together, He will be in our midst. If a church will worship together, He'll be in the midst of that congregation. *If the churches in a city will worship in unity, He'll be in the midst of that city!* His habitation is in our worship.

God wants to find a mercy seat on earth. He wants to dwell with us. If we can forge a mercy seat in our hearts and allow the pressures of life to put us in the right position, this is when God comes!

Our response to His presence—especially the response of our worship leaders and pastors—has much to do with determining whether God is going to just visit or stay and inhabit. Too often I have seen the pleading, the crying, the prayer meetings and watches where He does come; but just as quickly as He comes, His presence lifts. It's going to happen *right* somewhere, and there will be a *sustaining*. Then the place of greeting will become the place of meeting. There will come a people who, as pure worshipers, unified and beaten into place, will surround His throne with praise and worship. God will come and stay as long as worship has its wings outstretched over the centrality of Christ. The abandonment to worship will be like the Bible describes: The angels will cry one to another around the throne of God, saying, "Holy, Holy, Holy" (see Isa. 6:3). They don't know what else to say, because He who is seated before them is purer than the gold upon which He is seated.

Give yourself to the "tug" of God. When the Spirit prompts you, let Him tug your hands into position. Let Him bow your head. He is pulling you, saying, "Come on, you're almost there. Yield!" You just need to yield to become a worshiper.

Moms and dads, if you have trouble in your home, worship. It doesn't matter how serious the situation is with your kids.

God can solve it. Worship! Get together and worship over your home. Unite your arms outstretched in mercy over that home. Whatever is going on, I beseech you: Your kids don't need judgment; they need *mercy*. Unite in a sacrifice of worship and you can worship until God is literally attracted to your home and comes there for a place of habitation. Things will never be the same! His presence changes everything!

Pastors and people, do you want God to come to your church? Then begin to say, "I'm going to build a mercy seat. God, it's Your church. You lead. You guide and direct us. All we know how to do is worship." God will come.

When you are on the job, build that same seat for God to sit on according to the pattern that was given on the mountain. There is an elevation of worship that is coming to the Church, and we need it in the marketplace, the grocery store and the schools.

I don't know what it will take for some of us to see the reality of this. We get so focused on our problems instead of on *the reality of God and what He has promised.* He longs to come to us in glory and mercy. If God comes and sits in His glory and mercy, your problems are gone!

I challenge you: Begin right now. Worship God. Don't even ask for a blessing. *Mercy comes to those who make a mercy seat.* You won't have to ask for it. The days when we just seek out ministry for personal blessing are moving past. The Word of God says, "Bless the LORD, O my soul" (Ps. 103:1, *KJV*), not "O Lord, bless my soul!"

Begin building a mercy seat. Allow those hardened places of your heart to be lovingly beaten into place through worship so that your arms might be extended to welcome the Lord. As you do, you will cause others to run to this same mercy seat.

Go ahead, build a mercy seat for your children, for your city, for your work, for your family, for your home, for your marriage and for your church.

Seek His glorious face as you build this mercy seat and you *will* cause Him to come and remain! Pure, humble, unified worship is the earthly magnet that entices the Eternal One to a meeting place in time.

Hosting the Holy Spirit Through

CORPORATE PRAYER AND FASTING

by Lou Engle

Lou Engle is a man of prayer, passion and the prophetic. Lou has not only been a dear friend and a colaborer with me since 1984, but he has also been a prophet to me. A member of the apostolic team of Harvest International Ministries, Lou founded the 24-Hour House of Prayer at Harvest Rock Church, and he was the visionary behind The Call, where thousands of youth gathered on the Capitol Mall in Washington, DC, for united prayer and fasting.

In 1987 many members of Harvest Rock Church in Pasadena undertook extended fasts for 15 to 30 days. Nightly, our little band of fervent souls prayed with strong desire for the release of God's presence in our corporate worship. On the final Sunday of that period of fasting a prophetic song came forth in our midst. As the spontaneous words "We gaze into an open heaven" were sung, it was as if a bomb had exploded above us and the heavens opened. Pandemonium broke out. People began running, dancing, crying and shouting. One man began calling out, "I see angels!" Prophecy erupted among us. No one could preach. God had come!

The next season of our church life was one of high-level atmospheric intensity. People were saved and healed during worship. New songs were written. "First love" rested on the congregation. God had come in response to our spiritual desire expressed through earnest corporate prayer and fasting.[1]

SEASONS OF FASTING

Early in our years of church planting in California, the Lord led Pastor Ché Ahn and me to call for a season of corporate fasting each year during the month of January. Not everyone fasted for the entire month, but home groups would each fast on a designated week, during which their members would seek God for personal breakthrough and corporate revival. Inevitably, by the end of each January, God's presence would intensify over the congregation.

I will never forget the meetings where the fear of the Lord broke out among us. Ché began to minister in frighteningly clear words of knowledge and miracles of healing became a regular occurrence.

After a few years of this, I began to ask myself, *Why do we only do this in January?* The reward of being continually in God's presence seemed well worth the regular sacrifice and heart preparation of corporate fasting.

Jesus clearly said there is a reward in both corporate and individual fasting. In the Gospel of Matthew, Jesus declared:

When you [plural] fast, do not look somber as the hypocrites do, for they disfigure their faces to show men they are fasting. I tell you the truth, they have received their reward in full. But when you [singular] fast, put oil on your head and wash your face, so that it will not be obvious to men that you are fasting, but only to your Father who is unseen; and your Father, who sees what is done in secret, will reward you (Matt. 6:16-18, *NIV*).

This verse implies both a corporate and individual call to fasting. Jesus did not say *if* you fast but *when* you fast. Jesus expects His people to fast corporately with proper motivation. When we do, He will reward us. Charles Spurgeon, the great English preacher, understood the reward:

Our *seasons* of fasting at the tabernacle have been high days indeed; never has Heaven's gate stood wider; never have our hearts been nearer the central glory (emphasis added).[2]

I would like to advocate—no, rather, I believe the Holy Spirit would like to advocate regular seasons of corporate fasting and prayer in our local churches. Charles Finney, when faced with loss of spiritual power and dryness of soul, would withdraw for a day to fast and pray. Then the power would return. Our churches are also subject to spiritual decline. Regular seasons of fasting will help us return to the fire!

"Even now," declares the LORD, "return to me with all your heart, with fasting and weeping and mourning" (Joel 2:12, *NIV*).

Fasting is a God-given means for returning to our first love; it is a prescription for seeking Him with all our hearts. Hebrews 11:6 says, "He is a rewarder of those who diligently seek Him." In a culture dominated by pleasure seeking, isn't it time for the Church to give herself to regular seasons of God seeking? Our reward is Him!

Regular seasons of seeking His face are like spiritual chiropractic adjustments. They realign the members of the Body to the Head. The purpose of fasting is to align our hearts with God's heart. We are not trying to get something from God, so much as to realign our hearts, affections and priorities with His. Humility and hunger for God are the soil for the planting of His presence, and fasting is a way to prepare that soil.

Isaiah 58 reveals God's heart and promises concerning corporate fasting. If done with right motivation and outward expression of love for the world, God promises, "your healing will quickly appear" (Isa. 58:8, *NIV*). Corporate health can quickly be released to a church in a season of true humility and repentance expressed in fasting.

In biblical times the people of God adhered to regular God-called times of fasting. For instance, Paul kept the fast on the Day of Atonement. The Lord instituted public fasts for the well-being of His people:

> This is what the LORD Almighty says: "The fasts of the fourth, fifth, seventh and tenth months will become joyful and glad occasions and happy festivals for Judah" (Zech. 8:19, *NIV*).

Likewise, regular seasons of fasting in our local churches could be high days indeed of feasting on the presence of the Lord.

FIRST THE FAST, THEN THE FIRE

There is a difference between regular seasons of fasting and prophetic moments when God commands, "Tarry here in Jerusalem until you are endued with power" (see Luke 24:49).

The prophetic release to fast may come in the form of the clear voice of God or by a sovereign grace of supplication.

The Early Church, by the command of the resurrected Lord, first hosted the Holy Spirit with 10 days of united prayer, likely accompanied by fasting. The disciples were steeped in the revelation of Joel's prophecy. Peter explained the visitation by saying, "This is that which was spoken by the prophet Joel" (Acts 2:16, *KJV*). And what was Joel's prophecy? "Afterward, I will pour out My Spirit on all flesh" (Joel 2:28). Afterward? After what? After united prayer and fasting:

> Blow the trumpet in Zion, declare a holy fast, call a sacred assembly (Joel 2:15,16, *NIV*).

The established model was first the fast, then the fire. The early saints, under the direct command of Jesus, waited for the promise.

In more recent history, the saints in Los Angeles opened a portal to heaven in similar fashion. In 1906, the city of Los Angeles had been brought to a place of divine repentance. The spirit of grace was released on intercessors for fasting. It was a prophetic moment. William Seymour and his revival core seized the moment and fasted 10 days before the outpouring of the Spirit on Azusa Street. I believe we could witness another Azusa in our time if God's people would commit themselves to prayer and fasting.

Pastors and leaders must be sensitive to the call of the Holy Spirit when He releases divine grace for a corporate fast. Consider the preparation of the saints in North Battleford, Canada, prior to the great Latter Rain outpourings in 1948 and beyond. Franklin Hall had written a book in 1946 called *Atomic Power Through Fasting and Prayer*, which helped to ignite a revival of fasting in North America. Thousands went on extended fasts in America and Canada. The Latter Rain brethren in Canada had received the book and applied its teachings.

The fasting of the Latter Rain brethren was not a regular or planned fast but a divine moment in history. God breathed upon them the spirit of fasting. Hall's book was the voice of the Lord to them. Listen to their testimony:

> During the past six weeks we have enjoyed a great visitation of the Spirit of God. Some of us have been praying for twenty years that the nine gifts of the Spirit would be restored to the Church. The Spirit [of] fasting and prayer has rested upon the whole school all winter. Finally the great "Break Through" came and the spiritual gifts began to operate among us. . . . The revival is spreading all over the province.
>
> The truth of fasting was one great contributing factor to the revival. . . . Previously we had not understood the possibility of long fasts. The revival would never have been possible without the restoration of this great truth.[3]

One of the outstanding features of the Latter Rain revival was the "heavenly choir":

> Heaven's very strains filled the whole church. It was as a mighty organ, with great swelling chords, and solo parts weaving in and out, yet with perfect harmony. Those who heard it some blocks away said it did something to their souls that no power on earth had previously touched.
>
> Special healings were wrought: deaf heard, blind saw, cancers were healed and sick bodies made whole. Sinners were saved, and the precious blood of Jesus availed in it all.[4]

Clearly, there is a longing in the Church today for such a connection to heaven. In 1948 it was a God-breathed fast that opened the windows for the rain of heaven.

FASTING AND THE POWER OF HEALING

Irenaeus, an Early Church father, wrote, "For even among the brethren frequently as in the case of necessity when a whole church united in much fasting and prayers, the spirit has returned to the exanimated body, and the man was granted to the prayers of the saints."[5] The Early Church raised the dead with united prayer and fasting! The same can be done today!

The healing revivals that began in 1947 were directly linked to the move of fasting and prayer of that time. Men like T. L. Osborn and Oral Roberts later saw their healing ministries break out after seasons of fasting and prayer. More recently, Ja Shil Choi of the Full Gospel Prayer Mountain in Korea gave testimonies of great healings and deliverances through fasting and prayer in her book *Korean Miracles*.

I see a great day of healing power dawning for the churches of America and the earth, if only we will follow in the way of the Lord Jesus, who after 40 days of fasting came out of the wilderness "in the power of the Spirit" (Luke 4:14). Immediately, Jesus began to heal the sick and cast out demons, ministering in mighty authority and power to "those living in darkness and in the shadow of death" (Luke 1:79, *NIV*). Now we too are on the threshold of a great demonstration of signs and wonders after preparation in fasting.

FASTING FOR A NEW DAY

In January 1996, our church entered a 40-day season of fasting and prayer, stirred by the vision of Dr. Bill Bright. His call was for

2 million believers in North America to set themselves to 40-day fasts before the year 2000 to avert judgment and prepare to bring in the greatest harvest of souls in America's history. Christians across the nation answered that call.

Our season of fasting birthed a day-and-night House of Prayer at Harvest Rock Church. Even now the vision of 24-hour worship and prayer is being carried throughout Los Angeles and into the nations. As Houses of Prayer arise all over the earth, I believe a cloud of incense will cover the earth with the atmosphere of heaven. When this happens, we will see difficult things become simple and impossible things change. Fasting is an integral part of hosting the Holy Spirit in continual worship and prayer. Fasting changes hearts and changes cities.

At the dawn of a new millennium, we are seeing a new upsurge in fasting and the presence of the Holy Spirit among a very special group: the youth of our nation. I believe the youth of America are God's chosen instruments to bring radical revival in this hour.

Just as God has led Harvest Rock Church through a history of corporate prayer and fasting, He has also led us to call the youth of America to fasting, prayer and radical dedication to Christ. As I have been privileged to gather with these young people, I have seen the favor of God resting on their consecration and the Spirit of God hovering to birth a mighty youth revival in this nation.

BURNING PASSION ERUPTED FROM THE HEARTS OF THESE YOUNG TORCHES BEING FORMED AND FORGED IN THE FIRES OF FASTING.

I believe God is now releasing initiatives of this ancient tool of intercession and fasting to the next generation all over our land. In July 1999, more than 4,000 youth from most of the 50 states gathered in Colorado Springs for an event called PrayerStorm. The majority of the students fasted and prayed for three days, calling on God for a great youth awakening in America. What burning passion erupted from the hearts of these young torches being formed and forged in the fires of fasting!

Something is happening. A momentum is growing. A group of 25 youth in Seattle continued in daily fasting, and God moved. Their group grew to 625, and they are still growing. I see a new breed arising of young Christians like these. They are fasting, some for 40 days. They are praying. They are earnest about the presence of the Holy Spirit. They are turning their faces from television to God-vision.

On September 2, 2000, thousands of youth gathered on the Capitol Mall in Washington, DC, for a massive multigenerational fasting-and-prayer event known as The Call. Youth ministries and churches all across the nation heard the trumpet call and responded, coming to join their hearts and bend their knees for mercy, generational reconciliation and historic revival in America. I believe God intended this event to be a prophetic response to the tragedies at Columbine and schools throughout our land. Only God can offer the antidote to the violence and despair felt in this generation.

A CALL TO ALL

America's rich heritage of corporate fasting in times of crisis began with a Pilgrim people. William Bradford, in response to a drought that threatened crops, called a corporate fast for July 16, 1623. That very evening a steady, gentle rain soaked the crops, and in the fall an abundant harvest was brought in. Nearly four centuries later, a nation that has forsaken its heritage and lost its biblical moorings is returning to God by way of corporate fasting and repentance.

For such a time as this will the Holy Spirit honor our fasts. For such a time as this will God change hearts and heal families and generations. For such a time as this may we host the Holy Spirit through our humility and consecration.

Just as God showed mercy in response to the collective fasts of humility and repentance of Jehosaphat, Joel, Esther and Ninevah, He will respond to our corporate prayer and fasting by sending the Holy Spirit among us to do a new work today. May He come among us with widespread revival and once again align our hearts and land with the purposes of God!

Notes
1. Lou Engle, *Digging the Wells of Revival* (Shippensburg, PA: Destiny Image, 1998), p. 145.
2. R. D. Chatham, *Fasting* (Plainfield, NJ: Bridge Publishing, Inc., 1987), p. 93.
3. Richard M. Riss, *The Latter Rain* (Mississauga, Ontario, Canada: Honeycomb Visual Productions Ltd., 1987), p. 66.
4. Ibid., p. 82.
5. Chatham, *Fasting*, p. 79.

WORSHIP

by Ché Ahn

Ché Ahn is senior pastor of Harvest Rock Church in Pasadena, California, and he is president of an apostolic network, Harvest International Ministries. Ché is the author of Into the Fire, *a revealing personal account drawing on his intimate encounter with the Lord at the Toronto Blessing, his subsequent setbacks and, later, the miracles at Mott Auditorium, where Harvest Rock services are held.*

> *Thou art holy, O thou that inhabitest the praises of Israel.*
> PSALM 22:3, *KJV*

Truly, the Holy Spirit inhabits the praises of His people. In the *New King James Version*, the above passage reads, "But You are holy, enthroned in the praises of Israel." The word translated as "inhabit" from the Hebrew means to sit down, to remain, to settle or marry. God, in the person of the Holy Spirit, is not only attracted to the praises of His people but *promises to live and intimately abide in them*. What an inspiration to give ourselves completely to worship!

Worship is the encouraging adoration of who God really is and how He deserves to be praised. Someone once said that encouragement is oxygen to the soul. We all love sincere encouragement. In the same way, the Holy Spirit loves to "hang around" those who sincerely magnify, worship and glorify God. Worship is a tremendous way to rightly honor and host the Holy Spirit.

I believe that once the glory comes to a church and people hear that the glory of God is present in your midst, they will line up hours before a service begins just to experience time in His presence. Unbelievers, too, will come and give their hearts to Jesus. A clear illustration of how the presence of the Holy Spirit comes when we worship is found in the second book of Chronicles:

> The Levites who were the singers, all those of Asaph and Heman and Jeduthun, with their sons and their brethren, stood at the east end of the altar, clothed in white linen, having cymbals, stringed instruments and harps, and with them one hundred and twenty priests sounding with trumpets—indeed it came to pass, when the trumpeters and singers were as one, to make one sound to be heard in praising and thanking the LORD, and when they lifted up their voice with the trumpets and cymbals and instruments of music, and praised the LORD, saying: "For He is good, for His mercy endures forever," that the house, the house of the LORD, was filled with a cloud, so that the priests could not continue ministering because of the cloud; for the glory of the LORD filled the house of God (2 Chron. 5:12-14).

Once the glory comes—the manifest presence of the Holy Spirit—the rest is history! The priests of the Temple could not perform their duties because of the wonderful, weighty presence of the glory of God. The activities of man ceased, and all that was left was the Lord.

Worship invites the Spirit to come in glory and power. That is one reason why God is seeking worshipers.

THE HOLY SPIRIT SEEKS WORSHIPERS

In John 4, we see an interesting dialogue between Jesus and a Samaritan woman. The Samaritans and the Jews valued holy places and sites for the purpose of worship. The Jews championed Jerusalem; the Samaritans, Gerizim. But Jesus emphasized to the woman (and to us) that God does not bless a particular *site* but, rather, the *people* who worship Him in spirit and in truth, no matter what their location:

> But the hour is coming, and now is, when the true worshipers will worship the Father in spirit and truth; for the Father is seeking such to worship Him. God is Spirit, and those who worship Him must worship in spirit and truth (John 4:23,24).

We find three important insights in this passage. First, God will visit where there is true worship, regardless of the location. Whether you are in prison or in a magnificent cathedral, the Lord will honor and receive those who worship Him in spirit (man's spirit, albeit with the help of the Holy Spirit).[1]

Second, worship is not a passive pursuit on God's part. The word "seeking" is in the active present tense. This means that God places high priority on worship; He is actively and passionately seeking true worshipers.[2]

Finally, Jesus says that God is Spirit. God the Holy Spirit is seeking worshipers, as is God the Father. Thus by worshiping God in spirit and in truth, we also honor and welcome the Holy Spirit.

We get a very real glimpse into the truth of these words when Jesus visits the home of Mary and Martha (see Luke 10:38-42). Who is really hosting Jesus in this passage? In the natural, one would say Martha—a responsible hostess who is most likely preparing a lavish meal for the Rabbi. Mary was simply sitting at the feet of Jesus, listening to His words and responding with love, adoration and worship. Jesus commends Mary for giving Him what He desired. Good hospitality means meeting the true desires of your guest, not what you perceive his or her needs to be. Mary is the sister truly hosting Jesus in this passage.

When we are still and sitting at the feet of Jesus, attentively listening and seeking His face in worship (rather than busying ourselves with what we consider to be important), then we are truly hosting the Holy Spirit.

THE HOLY SPIRIT WANTS US TO SEEK HIS FACE

If my people, who are called by my name, will humble themselves and pray and seek my face and turn from their wicked ways, then will I hear from heaven and will forgive their sin and will heal their land (2 Chron. 7:14, *NIV*).

I have heard this verse taught and quoted in innumerable prayer meetings and services in recent years. Because we are hungry for revival, this verse has become a banner verse trumpeted through-out our land, and rightly so! But most of the time, we place the focus on humility, prayer and turning from our wicked ways without ever elaborating on the idea of seeking His face. I believe seeking God's face is an absolute condition for seeing revival in our day.

Seeking His face is different than seeking His hands. To seek His hands is to ask God for help or a sign. Just as a beggar will ask for help, hoping you will put your hands in your pockets and bring forth money, we often seek God's hands. But to seek God's face is to worship Him. It means listening to God, looking at His face in delight—not requiring of Him but seeking what is on His heart from the expression on His face. It means communicating your love and worship toward Him without thought of what you will receive in return.

Consider couples who are in love. They are often seen looking into each other's eyes. By looking at one's eyes, you can more intimately and completely communicate the love, fondness and adoration you have for your beloved.

The favor and presence of the Holy Spirit may come among us momentarily because we pray and ask for revival, but it is through intimate, selfless worship that He will abide.

This principle is powerfully illustrated by the visitation that came to Houston when my good friend Tommy Tenney was ministering there. Here is an account of what happened:

Tommy was a guest speaker at Christian Tabernacle, a multithousand-member Houston church where Pastor Richard Heard and many of the elders had been praying for revival for some years. On this particular morning, the worship and praise in the early service intensified to a level they had seldom felt or seen before. Tommy said it was like the bridal train in Princess Diana's wedding: It came, and then it kept on coming and coming.

The pastor turned to Tommy and asked if he was ready to speak. "To tell you the truth," he replied, "I'm half afraid to go up there. I think something is going to happen." The pastor said he felt he should read from Scripture and that he had a word from the Lord. Going up to their new high-tech, space-age, unbreakable acrylic pulpit, Pastor Heard opened his Bible to 2 Chronicles 7:14 and read aloud. "The word of the Lord to us is to stop seeking His benefits and seek Him. We are not to seek His hands any longer, but seek His face."

Then something happened that has since sent shock waves through the Church. Though there was no rain or lightning outside, there came a clap like thunder, and the pulpit Pastor Heard was standing in front of split in half. He was thrown back, knocked out on the floor, unable to move for hours. The pulpit was thrown forward, landing in two pieces in the carpeted altar area, forever unusable. The presence of God was so strong in the church that people arriving in the parking lot outside for the second service fell out of their cars as they opened the doors to get out. The meeting went on and on into the evening and the next day and continued week after week as people met God, were saved, delivered, healed and restored. It made an impression on Tommy he will never forget. When I asked him a year later what it was like, his eyes filled with tears. "I can scarcely speak about it," he said.[3]

THE HOLY SPIRIT IS RESTORING DAVIDIC WORSHIP

In Acts 15, James is speaking to the leaders of the church in Jerusalem when he quotes a very interesting passage from the book of Amos:

And with this the words of the prophets agree, just as it is written: "After this I will return and will rebuild the tabernacle of David, which has fallen down; I will rebuild its ruins, and I will set it up; so that the rest of mankind may seek the LORD, even all the Gentiles who are called by My name, says the LORD who does all these things" (Acts 15:15-18).

James and Amos are telling us that three things will happen: (1) God is going to restore David's fallen tent; (2) David's tent represents the pattern and passion of worship that God esteems; (3) as a result, Jewish believers (the remnant) will worship the Lord, and Gentiles also will come to Christ and worship Him.

What an incredible promise! If I understand this passage correctly, when the passion and pattern of Davidic worship is restored, the result will be Gentiles coming to Christ. This makes sense as we consider that worship brings the manifest presence or glory of God with it. When the glory comes, His presence will draw the Gentiles of the nations unto Christ. This is confirmed in Isaiah 40:5 (*NIV*): "And the glory of the LORD will be revealed, and all mankind together will see it."

You might ask, *What was so special about David's fallen tent? Why does God wish to restore it? Why not Solomon's Temple? After all, the glory fell once before during the dedication of Solomon's Temple. Why not the Tabernacle of Moses, the first model of worship for the Israelites?* As we study David's tent, we can better see why God so loved that tabernacle. First of all, David was a worshiper. Period. The Bible says that David was a man after God's own heart (see 1 Sam. 13:14).

Simply read the psalms that David wrote and you will see his passion and love for the Lord. The way David worshiped and the way he encouraged the people to worship gives us many clues about the type of worship God intends to restore in these last days.

David loved the Lord with a passionate, extravagant love, and he was not afraid to show it publicly. We see extravagant worship as the Ark of the Covenant was being brought up to Jerusalem.

> So David went down and brought up the ark of God from the house of Obed-Edom to the City of David with rejoicing. When those who were carrying the ark of the LORD had taken six steps, he sacrificed a bull and a fattened calf (2 Sam. 6:12,13, *NIV*).

This passage amazes me. I don't know how far Obed-Edom's house was from Jerusalem, but the fact remains that David took six steps with the Ark and then made a bull sacrifice—*every six steps!* Can you imagine all the bulls that were sacrificed? Can you fathom how long it took to get to Jerusalem this way? Regardless, David loved God with a passionate, extravagant and sacrificial love. With the restoration of David's tent will also come the restoration of this kind of love.

Dancing

David worshiped the Lord with his whole being, specifically expressed through dance. The Word of God tells us that David, wearing a linen ephod, "danced before the LORD with all his might" (2 Sam. 6:14). We are encouraged in Scripture to worship God with dance:

> Let them praise His name with the dance; let them sing praises to Him with the timbrel and harp (Ps. 149:3).

> Praise Him with the timbrel and dance; praise Him with stringed instruments and flutes! (Ps. 150:4).

With the restoration of David's tent will come a full restoration of worshiping God with dancing. In our church, we see the importance and the blessing of God on dance; we have a dance team that worships in dance every service. We also encourage the people to move out into the open spaces of our auditorium to express their love to God through dance. This may seem odd or different to some of our visitors; but what we are after is the presence of God. He delights in the abandonment of self in a dance of worship before Him. As I travel to churches around the world, I see the restoration of prophetic, expressive, worshipful dance.

Shouting

The Bible also has much to say about shouting:

> But let all those that put their trust in thee rejoice: let them ever shout for joy, because thou defendest them: let them also that love thy name be joyful in thee. (Ps. 5:11, *KJV*)

David and the entire house of Israel brought up the Ark of the Lord with shouts and the sound of trumpets (see 2 Sam. 6:15). Other references to shouting in the psalms include Psalms 32:11; 33:3; 35:27; 47:1,5; 60:8; 65:13; 66:1; 81:1; 98:4,6; 100:1; 132:9; and 132:16.

Even as I was writing this, I watched highlights of baseball great Mark McGwire hitting his 62nd home run of 1998, breaking the 37-year-old record of Roger Maris and causing Busch Stadium in St. Louis to erupt into bedlam—thousands of people shouting, clapping and cheering, and rightfully so. What I cannot understand is that although Jesus accomplished something infinitely greater when He died for our sins and rose again from the dead, providing redemption and salvation for us, many Christians think it is sacrilegious for us to shout for joy and clap our hands in thanksgiving during a church service! As someone once said, some churches would have us check our emotions at the door before we worship God in His house. Many people in these services look so unhappy and miserable, as though they were wearing underwear two sizes too small! Our churches need to get a life and worship God with shouts of praise and joy. I believe this is exactly what God is restoring through Davidic worship.

Musical Instruments

David also worshiped the Lord with instruments, specifically trumpets in 2 Samuel 6:15. Many additional Scripture passages encourage God's people to worship Him with instruments (e.g., see Pss. 33:2,3; 150). God is saying to use whatever talents you have in worshiping the Lord. Whatever you do, do all for the glory of God! (see 1 Cor. 10:31).

We are to love Him with all our hearts, our minds, our souls and our strength (see Luke 10:27), and we should express that love in passionate, extravagant worship. God welcomes the talents and skills of musicians, just as he welcomes unique expressions of worship from singers, dancers, sculptors, painters, bricklayers, homemakers, parents, etc. All these expressions reflect what God seeks: a life of worship in which we offer ourselves totally to God.

The most potent form of worship you can give is to offer your life daily as a sacrifice to Him. The Holy Spirit seeks the ongoing sacrifice of your life as an act of worship. The Bible makes it very clear just how deeply God wants us to commit ourselves to Him in worship:

I urge you, brothers, in view of God's mercy, to offer your bodies as living sacrifices, holy and pleasing to God—this is your spiritual act of worship (Rom.12:1, *NIV*).

Your body is the temple of the Holy Spirit who is in you . . . you are not your own. . . . For you were bought at a price; therefore glorify God in your body and in your spirit, which are God's (1 Cor. 6:19,20).

It is fitting that all we are to be rendered unto God as a living sacrifice, for Jesus exhorted us to render "to God the things that are God's" (Matt. 22:21).

Let us give ourselves in every way in worship to our heavenly Father. In doing this, we will attract the Holy Spirit so that He will be delighted to abide both in our lives and in our corporate assemblies.

Here are seven simple principles of worship to remember for maintaining a life of worship before Him:

1. PRESENT: Present your whole life to Jesus, continually. This is a true act of worship.
2. PRAY: Pray and ask God to make you a worshiper. Come to church services "prayed up."
3. PARTAKE: Partake of God's Word regularly as you worship.
4. PARTICIPATE: Participate regularly in corporate worship. Come on time with a right attitude to enter into worship.
5. PRAISE: Regularly praise Him and give Him thanks. Then enter into adoration and the intimacy of deep worship.

6. PRACTICE: Practice worship on your own with dance, singing, etc. Who you are alone with God is a true indicator of where you are in worship.

7. PERSEVERE: Persevere until you have encountered God. He will always come!

Notes

1. Leon Morris, *The New International Commentary on the New Testament: The Gospel According to John* (Grand Rapids, MI: Wm. B. Eerdmans Publishing, 1995), p. 270.
2. Ibid., p. 271.
3. Winkie Pratney, *Fire on the Horizon* (Ventura, CA: Regal Books, 1999), pp. 170, 171.

MINISTERING TO OUR YOUTH

by Winkie Pratney

When I was 19 years old (two years old in the Lord), Winkie Pratney invited me to his home in Texas. For two weeks he poured his life into me, and he has since become a lifetime friend and mentor. I know of no one else who has effectively reached the youth of this world for more than three decades. Winkie has worked with Campus Life, Champions for Christ, Operation Mobilization, Master's Commission, Youth With A Mission, Young Life, Youth Alive and Teen Challenge. He has written more than a dozen books including Fire on the Horizon: How the Revival Generation Will Change the World.

Let no one despise your youth, but be an example. . . .
Do not neglect the gift that is in you.
1 TIMOTHY 4:12-14

Perhaps the last words our world would use to describe today's younger generation are "cherished" and "gifted." Yet the Lord sees them as exactly that and more.

Our young people are the heirs of a new, exciting move of the Holy Spirit. They are the bold champions who will bring the gospel to the next generation. Indeed, they may even *be the* final generation! The bold extremism of today's youth, when channeled by God, offers the most exciting promise.

Will we, as those raised in the midst of a people consumed with selfishness, lovingly give away that which we have so freely been given? Will we esteem the young among us as more important than ourselves? Will we delight the Holy Spirit by embracing these sons and daughters as His highest gift and lavishing upon them their inheritance in God? How we treat, release and love our youth has much to do with causing the Holy Spirit to remain among us.

Allow me to offer some insight into the nature of these young men and women that will help us please God in our choices. Then let us respond to His call to launch this next generation into both His love and His destiny for them.

EMBRACING THE DIGITAL GENERATION

We call them many names, these young men and women. For better or worse—under God or under another—these youth will lead us into the future and shape the culture, customs and countries of the new millennium. There are real differences between the older and younger extremes of the youth generation now emerging, but they all share some characteristics in common as the young of tomorrow's world. For a number of reasons, I call them the Digital Generation, or Digitals.

Highly Visual
Of all generations throughout history, this is the most visually sophisticated of all time. They see things faster and more percep-

tively than their parents or grandparents; they are highly sensitive to tiny visual cues and body language clues from those they meet. Do not think you will easily fool Digitals, who have grown up watching the best actors working with incredibly sophisticated special effects. Any acting on our part, no matter how religiously practiced, will never be good enough to fake them out for any length of time. The Greek word for "hypocrite" is a word that meant an actor under an assumed character. We must be very real with this generation; if we are not, they will know.

Bill Gothard calls children "God's little spies." A primary ministry of the Holy Spirit is to lead us into all truth, for He is called the Spirit of truth (John 14:17). Digitals are not only sensitive to hypocrisy but are also genuinely hungry for reality. Anyone who would lead the Digital Generation or influence their lives must be deeply truthful in his or her own personal walk with God. We must live in unposed transparency, with genuine affection for these young men and women. It will not do for us to tell them we love them—we must *show* them.

Casually Technological

Digitals grew up with sophisticated technology and are no more deeply interested in the underlying structure of the technology (except perhaps to modify it) than a parent would be fascinated with the graphite categorization of a #2 pencil. It's usually the parents who ask admiring questions about computer details such as RAM, hard-drive capacities, processor speeds and the like. Digitals just want the stuff to do what they need it to do. As long as the equipment works, fine; they just want to get on with it.

Digitals are wholly comfortable with unfamiliar, cutting-edge tools, often in contrast to their parent's uneasiness with something new. Video games, worldwide Internet access, sophisticated simulations—digital technology is the native habitat of Digitals. While adults are impressed by technology, this bunch is interested only with what it does and what it can do for them.

We can actually shoot ourselves in the foot by trying too hard to impress our youth in this regard. The Holy Spirit can dazzle better than we can concoct; we need to remember this. As you reach out to youth or design their meeting spaces, don't go overboard on the technology or try to compete with what Hollywood does best.

Wide-screen video, tracking lasers and Austin Powers-type "groovy baby" mirror balls may be cute, but none of this counts in a visitation of God. Certainly, such sets must never be central. Technology in the modern world became modern man's Holy Spirit and science fiction modern man's prophecy; postmoderns know better now. *Unplugged* is the order of the hour.

BEFORE THERE WAS HIGH-DEFINITION VIDEO WITH DIGITAL SURROUND SOUND, GOD GAVE VISIONS. HE WANTS TO DO THE SAME TODAY.

Digitals are mildly amused by adult earnestness in seeking to provide relevance to the church environment; but remember that anything too glossy is suspect. "Better is a little with the fear of the LORD" (Prov. 15:16) and "Before honor is humility" (Prov. 15:33). The cup that is the true Holy Grail is never one of the jeweled pretenders to the throne standing prominently and glittering out front. A glitzy four-color tract or promo piece may not get the same read as something anointed which appears to be done on toilet paper and is hand illustrated in black and white.

The Holy Spirit is more than able to impress in an incomparable way, and one supernatural vision or other demonstration of His power can more than compensate for a high-definition video projection system with Dolby digital surround sound. Before we had video, God gave visions! He wants to do the same today!

We must remember to make room and make way for the supernatural with our youth. We must expect that God wants to move in His way. God knows what He is up against. He is not threatened by what kids find fascinating at the electronics store. What Ezekiel, John, Paul and Isaiah saw would blow away any cute or pretentious production we can ever dream up. We must use only the technology we really need so that these kids can clearly hear and see what we're showing them. Our funds are better spent on Bibles and training materials for the fruit of the revival.

Many Digitals who are totally comfortable with technology and the realms of fantasy are often wholly uncomfortable with people and practical society. That is why we—as parents, leaders and friends of this generation—must be genuinely personal. We should be fun to be with, accepting and constantly accessible, though we usually need to take the initiative. We need to lead in practical discipleship. This generation is more interested in a "Just Do It" kind of theology than any deep investigation of the meanings of the Greek word for "go." Digitals respond to real discipling—showing them how to do stuff, both in the Spirit and in their society. Jesus called the disciples to be with Him (see Mark 3:14) that He might send them out both to do and to teach (see Matt. 5:19).

Shamed

Digitals come from a society where there is no longer any real cultural guilt or genuine knowledge of the true God, and yet they seem to be blamed for everything that is wrong with our nation. When there is no acknowledged basis for guilt and when blame is so rampant that it is no longer effective, the only emotional consequence to perceived wrong is shame.

The Digital Generation is steeped in shame. They feel shame over not measuring up in clothing, class and cultural expectations; they feel awkward and alien and uncool among all except a carefully chosen company of few. Shame is central to Digital consciousness, often seeming to be the only remaining sanction to which they respond. Yet this is the one pressure we cannot afford to use. It is demoralizing and defeating. Jesus bore the shame of our failures and our missing the mark so that we wouldn't have to. He was stripped naked and hung, disfigured and beaten, in front of a mocking crowd—precisely for the purpose of taking our place (see Heb. 12:2). We must never seek to shame those called to His inheritance. We must honor the Lord and win them through love and acceptance.

During the Jesus Movement of the 1970s, the late Dr. Francis Schaeffer met a bedraggled hippie in a Christian meeting. The young man came to see him, full of fear and anticipating rejection. Schaeffer simply embraced him and said, "Welcome!"

"Why did you say that?" exclaimed the astonished kid.

"Because I know who you are" he replied.

"I don't even know who I am," said the boy. "How do you know who I am?"

Schaeffer responded, "You are made in the image of God and are precious and unique to Him. Therefore you are most welcome."

Shame is not an option for any kind of ministry or outreach bearing the name of our Lord. Digitals must be embraced, honored as humanity and forgiven for failure. Grace must be cried to the mountain and mercy to the throne (see Zech 4:7; Heb. 4:16). Salvation, healing, revival—all such acts of God find their ultimate ground in His mercy. Why should embracing these youth be any different?

Scattered

Digitals feel orphaned, abandoned and, often, utterly alone. They are the survivors of the worst holocaust in Western history. One-third of Generation X never even made it out of the womb; more than 16 million were killed by their own parents. Another 16 million were forced to somehow survive the worst fear of any kid in this generation: to see your family broken up and destroyed.

The aftermath of all this destruction is all around our young people and written into the DNA of their culture. This DNA reads that nobody really wants you—people are concerned for themselves. They want you out of their lives and on your own. Forming tribes for self-protection and comfort, Digitals are hungry for some kind of genuine love and mutual acceptance. At heart they have the same desires we all have: to be part of something real, something close—a family. We would do well to reach out as family—whether we are or not—and understand and incorporate the biblical model of adoption and covenant (see Deut. 7:9; 29:9-15; Rom. 8:14-17; 9:3-8).

We can't ask this generation to behave as we want them to or even to behave as Christians—to toe the line merely because we say they should. If we first truly treat our youth as family, they may then be mobilized as an army for God.

Scorned and Rejected

To many adults, Digitals are the twenty-first century lepers and are often treated as such. The media does nothing to counter this charge. Coverage of recent violence in schools, vicious gang initiations that spill out into society, and children killing their own parents (usually because of intractability in their homes) has caused our youth to become feared as destroyers. There is nothing that terrifies people more than that which is utterly "other," or foreign, to them. That is why the presence of the Lord by His Spirit brings the fear of the Lord (see Isa. 2:21)—and such an alarming reaction where we might fall down as dead (see Rev. 1:17).

By comparison, this generation of youth—being perceived as alien—can too easily be met with the catastrophic reaction of rejection. Rejection breeds contempt and scorn—scorn born of suspicion, alienation and hatred.

Perceived through the lens of a differing generational expectation, many Digitals are wholly strange to their parents and pastors and fellow congregants. Sometimes these differences are so strong that Digitals are perceived by their elders as total misfits and subsequently discarded as practically useless.

Yet God has always seen fit to choose and use those seen as poor and powerless to build the Kingdom (see 1 Cor. 1:18-31). Digitals must feel the chosenness of their unique calling, their specialness by the election of God (see 1 Pet. 2:4; Rev. 17:14). Before the fire of faith can fall upon our churches, kids must first be brought into the light of hope. Biblical hope makes us not ashamed (see Rom. 5:5) and brings boldness to the missionary and the martyr to magnify Christ by life or by death (see Phil. 1:20).

No matter what their appearance or compatibility with our comfort zones, Digitals have a deep need to be accepted in the Beloved. They need to be lovingly welcomed because they are believers, and they must be trusted as future builders.

Understand, these young people are really special. On this generation has fallen the consciousness of a critical end-point in revival history. God has waited a long time for a people like this. This is a day when the lepers take the city (see 2 Kings 7:8)! Some of these outcasts will become missionaries of the one-way ticket and have a destiny as martyrs. Many will be those with nothing to lose. Having already lost it all, these kids will find in Christ and in the purposes and promises of His kingdom an abandoned life that changes history forever.

We must call them forth as the chosen of God and see them prophesied to as missionaries. They must be valued as truly worthy to receive the passing of the torch, just as Joshua was called to step into the place of Moses at the edge of the Promised Land.

Discouraged

Digitals are easily discouraged, because so many of them feel wholly overwhelmed by the terrible stresses and pressures placed on their lives in these modern times. School, peer pressure (sex, drugs, drinking, smoking), family, techno-stress, finances, fear of physical crime, the pressure of political correctness—all these things contribute to the relentless pressure they feel.

Digitals are drowning in a sea of tension. Because of constant pressure to perform, conform and survive, Digitals need to be constantly encouraged. They need to see their lives and futures called to bravery, and they must be continually ministered to for release into their own ministry. We must be like the Holy Spirit in that regard in our affirming love. The Holy Spirit stands by our side and calls us on to action and courage, all the while helping. That is His ministry. He is the Comforter, a Word filled with power and action (see John 14:16,26; 16:7, KJV). We can be part of that same place of refuge and life for this younger generation.

GOING TO EXTREMES

If there is one thing that makes people genuinely concerned about Digitals, it is this: Once their minds are made up about something, they seem willing to go to the extreme for it. Their games, dress, language and lifestyle all reflect this go-for-it, all-or-nothing, there-is-no-tomorrow attitude. Once committed to a course, they appear to have no reservation for self-preservation.

This all-or-nothing approach to everything is truly significant. Digital culture has produced Digital perception; there seems to be little sense of the gradual, the slow pace of the quietly growing process that we have known as life. Digitals often appear to have no volume control; everything they do demonstrates this same flat-out manner. And this very extremism can be used by the Holy Spirit and perceptive believers to help mold a radical and willing generation into something most precious.

The truth of God calls for a holy life in which there are genuine absolutes and real rights and wrongs. Digitals live in a postmodern culture that has no boundaries and no lasting realities, where fantasy is part of everyday actuality. Yet, at heart, this generation is hungry for a word that makes a difference—a message which is in itself a Digital message. They are the perfect recipients of an extreme, uncompromising call to holiness and truth. God has waited a long time for such a people.

As believers, we are called to come alongside to encourage, equip and empower these Digitals. We have a rare privilege, indeed, and a welcomed invitation to host the Holy Spirit by doing just that.

Hosting the Holy Spirit Through

EVANGELISM

by Ché Ahn

You shall receive power when the Holy Spirit has come upon you; and you shall be witnesses to Me in Jerusalem, and in all Judea and Samaria, and to the end of the earth.

ACTS 1:8

One of the most exciting ways we can host the Holy Spirit in our homes and churches is through reaching souls for Jesus Christ. The Holy Spirit will come and favor us in a particularly strong measure with His presence in power when we speak of Him to those who are lost.

As we are seeing in this book, there are many wonderful ways to host the Holy Spirit among those who are saved. But consider our Great Commission from the Lord: "Go into all the world and preach the gospel to every creature" (Mark 16:15). If the end purpose of our faith and our relationship with Jesus is to share Him with a perishing world, can you think of anything the Holy Spirit will more delight in than coming to enable our obedience to the highest call?

The Holy Spirit, according to Scripture, remains with us as the presence of the Lord until He returns again. The Holy Spirit comes alongside us and draws those who do not know Jesus into relationship with Him and brings them eternal life. This is the ultimate purpose for which Christ died. To deny the Lord access to our hearts and the eternal souls of others through failing to evangelize is perhaps the worst way we can offend the Holy Spirit and make Him feel unwelcome.

The burden of consigning the unsaved to a life of torment in hell is all too real to the Spirit. We need to see the Great Commission from God's perspective. Hell is real. It is eternal. It is horrible. The joy of life everlasting in Christ Jesus is just as real, but your witness is the bridge in that gap. We need to remember what a life without the Holy Spirit would be like.

Charles Finney said if you want God to give you a burden for souls, imagine looking through a telescope and seeing your loved ones suffering in hell. No matter what a person may suffer on Earth, it can never compare with the torment of hell. Now imagine those same loved ones in heaven—and how happy and free they could be with Jesus. No wonder the Holy Spirit is ready to empower you right now to be His witness! God is not willing that any should perish (see 2 Pet. 3:9). That is why I believe God gives even more power to those who are committed to obeying the Great Commission. No matter at what level you begin to obey, God will honor His principles: If you are faithful with little, you will be given much (see Luke 19:17).

Let's look at other passages that describe the Holy Spirit's role in evangelism. Luke 4:18 tells us that the Spirit is given for the purpose of preaching the good news and freeing the captives. In Acts 10:38, we see that the Holy Spirit's anointing was given to Jesus and, by extension, is given to us to do good and to heal those oppressed by the devil. The Holy Spirit's presence is not just for our enjoyment or pleasure or for falling down under His presence, but He comes so that we can go and do the works that Jesus did (see John 14:12)!

The Father sent Jesus to preach the gospel, heal the sick and cast out demons. Jesus then commissioned us to do the same: "As the Father has sent Me, I also send you" (John 20:21). When He said this, Jesus breathed on His disciples to receive the Holy Spirit (v. 22)!

OUR CENTRAL MISSION

The fruit of salvation is not the only reason God has called us to share the good news. By our obedience, we bring joy, honor and glory to God. We also bring life to ourselves and our churches. Missionary evangelist T. L. Osborn once said, "The holiest experience you can have with Christ is to lead a person to Christ."

Billy Graham admonished, "Evangelism is the central mission of the Church. Without it, believers become introspective and lacking in purpose, growth stagnates, worship becomes superficial, and selfishness stifles a spirit of giving."[1] The consequences of disobedience are far more grave than a lessened presence of the Holy Spirit; in fact, they lead to spiritual death!

God chooses to bless those people and churches who honor the Holy Spirit through evangelization and preaching the gospel. For those who do there is great reward now and for all eternity.

Here are five action points that have proven effective in my life and that of our church body for sharing Jesus and thus hosting the Holy Spirit.

Intercede

Argentine evangelist Carlos Annacondia, who has led more than 2 million souls to the Lord, has said that sharing the gospel could be likened to the Americans' military strategy in the Gulf War. Our bombers were sent in first to gain the victory before the ground troops arrived on the scene. Similarly, intercessory prayer strikes a winning blow for souls and evangelism gathers the results.

Our first prayer in an evangelistic effort should be to bind the god of this age who has blinded the mind of the unbeliever; then we must ask the Father to draw the unbeliever to salvation (see John 6:44; 2 Cor. 4:4).

Intercede with travail for your friends and relatives (see Acts 10:1,2). Prayer walk your community and claim souls, schools and businesses for Christ. Pray for your city. Claim the youth. By 2005, the teen population of our nation is expected to explode from 24 million to more than 35 million. Campus Crusade for Christ reports that 88 percent of them do not go to church; and of the 12 percent who do, most will not continue to attend church once they finish high school. According to Latin American revivalist Omar Cabrera, "Revival without touching the youth is no revival at all."[2]

Let us move with the winds of the Spirit today that are creating hunger and desperation in hearts across the world and allowing unprecedented access to share the gospel.

Invite

Invite people to your church services. This is one of the easiest things you can do. Ninety percent of people asked say they are open to visiting a church service if invited. Take advantage of holidays and special services. Invite foreign students and the unsaved for dinner or festivities at your home. There are more than 550,000 international students in the United States alone! Write a personal tract about your salvation experience and give it away to people you meet. Set a goal to win a certain number of people to the Lord in the coming year.

Involve
Get involved in the lives of non-Christians. Jesus was a friend of sinners and tax collectors. He got into other people's boats. Just as Jesus got into Peter's boat, we need to go and hang out where the lost meet—in their homes and neighborhoods and malls. We need to quit complaining about the world and do something about it. If you don't salt meat as it cures, the meat will eventually stink. If we don't salt the earth, it too will stink. Get involved in outreaches from your church and other organizations in your community, particularly those serving the poor and helping the homeless.

Introduce
Introduce people to Jesus. Bill Bright, founder of Campus Crusade, says that whenever he is with a person for more than 20 minutes, he feels it is an appointment by God to share the gospel. The Word tells us, "How shall they believe in Him of whom they have not heard? And how shall they hear without a preacher?" (Rom. 10:14). In other words, it takes a real human being sharing the good news for salvation to occur.

This need not be a difficult or complicated encounter, just sharing what you know from the heart. Nevertheless, many people don't share their faith because they think they don't know how. If this is where you stumble, read a book or two on evangelism, or take a class or seminar. The skills you gain will last for a lifetime, and the benefit to those with whom you share will last for eternity! So step out in faith and speak. God will always meet you, no matter how awkward you may feel.

Incorporate

An important final step in evangelizing is to incorporate the new believer into the Church. Birthing a baby without caring for it is not responsible. Likewise, we must bring new babes in Christ into the local church so that they may be cared for by the family of God and grow through nurturing relationships.

The archbishops of England wrote in 1918 that evangelizing is not complete until a man or woman will serve Jesus as Lord in the fellowship of His Church.[3] I like that definition! I believe it best captures God's intent. Of course, this means you must be a committed and active member yourself to best direct others to do the same. Give yourself to the harvest by helping and supporting your church and each of its vital outreaches—and by lovingly bringing new converts into the fold.

One final thought as to how best to share your faith. Someone once said, "Get on fire for God, and people will come to watch you burn!" Pursue Him, and sharing your faith will be the natural overflow.

Notes
1. Sterling W. Huston, *Crusade Evangelism and the Local Church* (Minneapolis, MN: World Wide, 1984), p. 67.
2. Source unknown.
3. C. Peter Wagner, *Strategies for Church Growth: Tools for Effective Mission and Evangelism* (Ventura, CA: Regal Books, 1987), p. 128.

UNITY AND A VISION FOR YOUR CITY

by Frank Damazio

In today's world the tendency to be self-focused extends to the attention we place on our own churches to the exclusion of the well-being of other churches and even our cities. In the Old Testament, the Lord spoke to Israel as a corporate people. Whether we are leaders or congregants, every believer is called by God to seek the well-being of the city to which he is called and to be a part of the body of believers in that place. The Holy Spirit is delighted to come and dwell among such unity and love. Allow your vision to be increased as you read Frank Damazio's exhortation about the significance of our cities—places in which the Holy Spirit longs to dwell! This chapter is adapted with permission from chapter 13 of Frank's book, Crossing Rivers, Taking Cities *(Ventura, CA: Regal Books, 1999). Frank Damazio is a friend, and he is senior pastor of City Bible Church in Portland, Oregon.*

Thus says the Lord GOD: "On the day that I cleanse you from all your iniquities, I will also enable you to dwell in the cities, and the ruins shall be rebuilt."

EZEKIEL 36:33

My relationship with my city is in many ways like the relationship I have with my wife: It's constantly growing. I loved her when we got married; but the more I know about her hidden personality, her unique giftings and her stalwart character, the more I love her. My love grows as our relationship grows and we experience more of life together—home, children, sorrow, pain, joy, disappointment, challenges and surprises.

When a pastor is called to a city, the bonding process is uniquely parallel to a romance, a marriage, a deepening relationship—a trying relationship! You may have experienced love at first sight for your city, or it may have been less than love, even disdain or disgust. Maybe you were trapped, snared, captured by circumstances: a word from God, a family situation or just going there for a little while and then moving on. A pastor's love for his city has a great deal to do with city reaching and city ministry.

THE MARRIAGE BETWEEN CHURCH CALL AND CITY CALL

If you were asked outright, "Do you love your church?" the answer most likely would be yes—but, of course, not without pain, sorrow, disappointment, glory days and gory days. But your love is real. The love for your city must be just as real and just as enduring. All cities have weaknesses and strengths and reasons people love it and hate it there: the weather, traffic, population size, atmosphere, smell, ethnic mix, educational limitations. Any or all of these factors could be reasons why you love or tolerate your city.

If God has called you to your church, He has called you to your city. Our vision begins not only with our church's future but also with our city's future. When you read the newspaper or listen to the news, do you find yourself listening with no interest, no real feelings, about such city problems as murders, rapes, burglaries, drownings, bankruptcies or laws passed that are blatantly against God's Word? Does your heart response sound like this: *Whatever! The world is certainly messed up. I can't believe our politicians. There is no respect for God in our city! Well, let's see, what should I preach on Sunday? Ah, now this is more like it, preaching to the church.*

Such a complacent response is exactly why many of us who are spiritual leaders need a revival in our souls concerning our love and pastoral concern for our cities. God loves the people in your church and in your city. God desires to disciple cities, shape cities and pastor the people in our cities. Yet we pastors and spiritual leaders have not been taught to love our cities as much as we love our churches.

LOVING YOUR CITY WHILE LOVING YOUR CHURCH

Permit me to share a little personal history here. My journey as a Christian leader seeking to be equipped for the ministry took me through Bible college, three seminaries, numerous conferences, seminars and other modes of education. I have a Bachelor of Theology degree, a Master of Divinity degree from Oral Roberts University and doctoral studies at both Fuller Seminary and ORU. In all my hundreds of hours of classes, I did not have one full class—that is, two or three credits—on the relationship between the city and the pastor: how to love the city, pastor in the city, network in the city, be involved with city life, meet the social needs in the city, minister to the youth of the city, et cetera.

Many books offer ample material on pastoral ministry and yet never mention the pastor and the city, let alone how to reach the city. We have been somewhat trained in preaching, teaching, counseling, prayer, administration, how to study, how to speak and how to run programs. But what happens to the city? Books abound on the subjects of ethical conduct, the pastor's wife, Sunday morning worship, midweek prayer meetings, evangelistic meetings, altar calls, dedications of infants, wedding ceremonies, funerals, ordination, finances, building programs and praying for the sick. But what happened to the city?

Is there really any question as to why most leaders and most churches are consumed with their own churches, having little or no contact with the outside world? Why is evangelism so difficult in the twenty-first-century Church? Because we are not in the city and the city is not in us. We have removed the candlestick from the city. We've removed the light, the oil, the ministry of Christ in and to the city. However, our first calling is not to the one congregation we preach to but to the whole city God has placed us in.

In Luke 10:1, we read that Jesus appointed 70 leaders to go two by two into every city and place where He Himself was about to go. God has appointed you and sent you into your city because *God is coming to your city*. He sent you to prepare a way for His presence and power to be released in your city. Jesus' heart for the city is revealed in Luke 19. Jesus is still outside of Jerusalem as He utters His lament, recorded only by Dr. Luke, a leader with deep feelings for his city:

Now as He drew near, He saw the city and wept over it, saying, "If you had known, even you, especially in this your day, the things that make for your peace! But now they are hidden from your eyes. For days will come upon you when your enemies will build an embankment around you, surround you and close you in on every side, and level you, and your children within you, to the ground; and they will not leave in you one stone upon another, because you did not know the time of your visitation" (Luke 19:41-44).

EVERY CITY HAS SPIRITUAL SEASONS

Jesus was the answer Jerusalem was seeking, but Jerusalem didn't know that. Jesus was the peace this city of tension and heartache needed but had failed to find. The very name Jerusalem meant city of peace. Its day of visitation had come, but the people could not recognize it. Jesus saw beyond the day; He saw the devastation coming—the future of the city—and He wept.

As leaders sent to our cities, we must be aware that there are prophetic moments, turning points, in our cities. When the turning point is missed, the future of the city is at stake. Jesus was the prophet who could foresee and the priestly intercessor who could intercede. His heart was burdened and His vision for the city would not diminish, even though the future would be devastating. Every city has a future, a destiny, a hope. We are to weep with God over our city's future.

Jesus speaks emphatically about the promised visitation for the city of Jerusalem: "You did not know the time of your visitation." The time of visitation is set by God but must be discerned by the city leadership. In this case, the visitation came to an indifferent city and in their indifference the people missed the time. Their obstinate resistance to Jesus would ultimately bring the city to ruin and overthrow the entire nation. The contrast between what was and what might have been was so great that Jesus could not refrain Himself from lamentation. He wept over His city. God will visit our cities either in revival and redemptive restoration or in judgment.

Our hope is that God would come to our cities to bless, to restore and to deliver. Failure to know the time of visitation is followed by definite grave consequences: a spiritual deadness that cannot be remedied without a shaking, a judgment or a time of spiritual barrenness.

Seasons of Sowing and Reaping

As a spiritual leader in my cities—we reach two cities, Portland, Oregon, and Vancouver, Washington, because they are geographically set together—I must have a heart and a vision for the visitation of God to the city. I believe the cities of today have a tremendous receptivity to the true gospel; our cities are full of opportunity. Cities, like individuals and nations, are subject to seasons, specific times to sow seed and specific times to reap the harvest.

What is the spiritual climate, the spiritual season of your city? Ted Haggard refers to the spiritual climate as knowing the water level of your city: "In the same way that water levels in a reservoir change according to the time of year or amount of rainfall, so cities and regions experience varying levels of the Holy Spirit's activity."[1]

I call this Holy Spirit activity "sowing and reaping seasons." I will reap where I have not sown and sow where I cannot reap. It doesn't matter. What really matters is that someone reaps and reaps well at the right time. When you are pastoring for the city and not just for the church, sowing and reaping takes on a whole new perspective.

IF WE ARE TO
REACH A CITY,
IT WILL TAKE THE
WHOLE CITY
CHURCH
TO REACH THE
WHOLE CITY.

We claim Acts 18:10: "I have many people in this city." Enough people to overflow hundreds of churches by 10 times their present church size. Let us not be concerned about our own church growth but with the overall growth of the city Church. Jesus had compassion for the multitudes. City reaching is the ability to see all the people in the city in search of the living God. The multitudes are there, but can we see them? I must embrace the simple fact that if we are to reach a city, it will take the whole city Church to reach the whole city.

A NEHEMIAH ATTITUDE

Each individual spiritual leader in the city must nurture a Nehemiah attitude—a passionate and persevering heart to reach our cities for God. Jerusalem was a thousand miles away from Nehemiah's world. To journey from his world, his lifestyle and his job security through dangerous country with hostile enemies and robbers required quite a commitment from Nehemiah. Why would a man leave his comfort zone for a burned-out, broken-down, devastated city? The answer is that he loved his city! To leave your palace and move to a city that offers nothing but work, warfare and weakness, you must have a vision for that city.

As a city-reaching, city-restoring strategist, Nehemiah is a model for all leaders who have a vision for their cities. Nehemiah had a deep spiritual burden for the condition of his city and a vision to change it:

> I asked them concerning the Jews who had escaped, who had survived the captivity, and concerning Jerusalem. And they said to me, "The survivors who are left from the captivity in the province are there in great distress and reproach. The wall of Jerusalem is also broken down, and its gates are burned with fire." So it was, when I heard these words, that I sat down and wept, and mourned for many days; I was fasting and praying before the God of heaven (Neh. 1:2-4).

NEHEMIAH'S PRAYER FOR THE CITY

When Nehemiah heard the state of his city, his response was four months of fasting, praying, weeping and mourning. The biblical description of how the city was devastated by King Nebuchadnezzar is found in 2 Chronicles 36:18,19:

> And all the articles from the house of God, great and small, the treasures of the house of the LORD, and the treasures of the king and of his leaders, all these he took to Babylon. Then they burned the house of God, broke down the wall of Jerusalem, burned all its palaces with fire, and destroyed all its precious possessions.

The magnificent place where God's glory was once displayed and respected by all nations was destroyed. The city lay in ruins, the Temple in pieces, and the people were taken into Babylonian captivity.

This is an accurate description of cities today around the world. Destroyed by moral perversity, disease, corruption, violence, worship of other gods, idolatry, occultism, pornography, abortion, euthanasia, child molestation, spousal abuse, discouragement, suicide, poverty, addictions—our cities have been sacked by the kingdom of darkness.

In *Loving Your City into the Kingdom*, Jack Hayford speaks of his Holy Spirit encounter during prayer when he was shown that his city was being destroyed. The Spirit revealed to him:

> You are not being told "Los Angeles will be destroyed," because this city is *already* being destroyed. It does not need a catastrophic disaster to experience destruction because the Destroyer is already at work. The toll you have recounted, which a severe earthquake might cost, is small in comparison to the reality that stalks this city every day.
>
> *More* than mere thousands are being speared through by the shafts of hell's darts, seeking to take their souls. *More* than 150,000 homes (not merely houses) are being assailed by the sin and social pressures that rip families and marriages apart. *More* havoc is being wreaked by the invisible grindings of evil power than tectonic plates could ever generate. A liquefaction of the spiritual foundations that alone allow a society to stand is wiping out the underpinnings of relationships, of righteous behavior and of healthy lifestyle.
>
> You are to pray against THIS—the present, ongoing, devastating destruction of the city of Los Angeles.[2]

But God is not going to allow our cities to continue under the principalities and powers of evil. God is raising up Nehemiahs who will leave the world of religious matters, job security, running church programs and running church committees to rebuild our cities. God stirred up a heathen named Cyrus, king of Persia, to restore the city of Jerusalem and rebuild the house of God. He released God's people to accomplish the vision:

> Now in the first year of Cyrus king of Persia, that the word of the LORD by the mouth of Jeremiah might be fulfilled, the LORD stirred up the spirit of Cyrus king of Persia, so that he made a proclamation throughout all his kingdom, and also put it in writing (2 Chron. 36:22).

Nehemiah was one of three key leaders to respond: first Zerubbabel, then Ezra and, finally, Nehemiah. Nehemiah was the king's cupbearer, a trusted prestigious position, before he became Nehemiah the city reacher and city rebuilder. Nehemiah's response to the challenge of reaching a city was prayer and fasting. Always begin with prayer and fasting. Before you strategize, before you program, before you engage the enemy—pray!

Nehemiah prayed 11 important prayers:

- Intercessory prayer for God's house (Neh. 1:9-11)
- Prayer before the king (Neh. 2:4)
- Prayer to overcome discouragement (Neh. 4:4,5)
- Prayer for divine protection (Neh. 4:9)
- Prayer for personal needs (Neh. 5:19)
- Prayer for inner strength (Neh. 6:9)
- Prayer against opposition (Neh. 6:14)

- Prayer for the vision (Neh. 13:14)
- Prayer for the mercy of God (Neh. 13:22)
- Prayer for spiritual leaders (Neh. 13:29)
- Prayer for God's blessing (Neh. 13:31)

Nehemiah's vision for the city aroused in him a desire to ask the Lord to send him to meet the need (see Neh. 2:15; Isa. 49:10,11). He was motivated to go and spy out the land first-hand (see Neh. 2:13-18) and then to strategize. Nehemiah was tested, attacked, accused and faced with impossible odds; yet without delay or distraction, he finished the work of rebuilding the city (see Neh. 6:15).

Nehemiah faced Sanballat and Tobiah, his first opposition, as will every city leader:

When Sanballat the Horonite and Tobiah the Ammonite official heard of it, they were deeply disturbed that a man had come to seek the well-being of the children of Israel (Neh. 2:10).

Nehemiah resisted the opposition and continued with his eye on the vision: rebuild the city. There will always be Sanballats and Tobiahs! Don't let the enemy use people as distractions to get you off course. Stay on course with your eye on the goal: the city. Nehemiah was able to unite the people of God to work together in the reaching of the city.

In Nehemiah 3, the leaders were united together in order to rebuild the city. The key phrases in this chapter are "next to," "next to them" and "next to him." These indicate that a team spirit existed as they built the city. Every leader had a part of the city to work on, and every leader had a specific responsibility. The leaders were knit together in one spirit, one vision and one heart. All was for the city, not their own personal gain, not their own houses; their only motivation was for the vision of a rebuilt city.

The city Church must work together to impact a city, every congregation building on different parts of the wall, every congregation standing next to, with, alongside and together in our ministry to the city. The knitting together of the leaders' hearts is first, then the congregations' hearts, and finally a unified city ministry can take place. We must pray that the Holy Spirit will touch the eyes of the city Church to see this vision of unified city ministries (see Matt. 9:29,30; Luke 24:31; Eph. 1:18). The Church can change the city instead of the city changing the Church.

CITY CHURCH PROCLAMATIONS

As a city Church, our desire to reach the city together necessitates city Church goals. The following are proclamations to make when setting out to take your city:

1. As a city Church, our desire is to build strong and spiritually healthy local churches with spiritual armories so together we can penetrate the spiritual powers over our city.

> The LORD has opened His armory, and has brought out the weapons of His indignation; for this is the work of the Lord GOD of hosts in the land of the Chaldeans (Jer. 50:25).

2. As a city Church, our desire is to reap the harvest God would grant us from our city metro area and region, using every means available or necessary to accomplish this.

Then He said to His disciples, "The harvest truly is plentiful, but the laborers are few. Therefore pray the Lord of the harvest to send out laborers into His harvest" (Matt. 9:37,38).

3. As a city Church, our desire is to mobilize all believers throughout our city and region to pray, fast, prayerwalk and unite together to minister mercy to every house, apartment and business within our targeted area, thus reaching our whole city.

For this purpose the Son of God was manifested, that He might destroy the works of the devil (1 John 3:8).

4. As a city Church, our desire is to penetrate every pocket or stronghold of darkness by increasing our repentance; first denying all sins revealed and then increasing our power of prayer intercession over our city and region (see Gen. 18:22,23; Isa. 59:16).

So I sought for a man among them who would make a wall, and stand in the gap before Me on behalf of the land, that I should not destroy it (Ezek. 22:30).

5. As a city Church, our desire is to help restore the inner city by reaching individuals with the gospel of Christ, seeing authentic conversions that result in new lifestyles, new life habits and rebuilding inner-city churches that will reap and keep the harvest.

Those from among you shall build the old waste places; you shall raise up the foundations of many generations; and you shall be called the Repairer of the Breach, the Restorer of Streets to Dwell In (Isa. 58:12).

6. As a city Church, our desire is to oppose abortion, moral perversity, homosexuality, pornography, prostitution (all moral sins that violate God's laws) by being salt and light with political involvement as is necessary, taking responsibility for our city region laws, not by political activism only, but also by aggressive intercession.

> Son of man, I have made you a watchman for the house of Israel; therefore hear a word from My mouth, and give them warning from Me (Ezek. 3:17).

Ted Haggard speaks wisely in his book *Primary Purpose* about Christians and political involvement:

> I believe that as responsible citizens, Christians should be involved in political issues. Even though we will be divided on most issues, there will be times when we will stand together. Some battles we will win, others we will lose. But the battle that must not be lost is the eternal struggle to liberate individuals spiritually, which will result in inspiring the whole community. In the midst of any political situation, we must stay steady and keep focus on our primary purpose, making it hard to go to hell from our cities.[3]

7. As a city Church, our desire is to reach each generation with the power of the gospel, reaching past, present and future generations with relevant spiritual tools and methods. We commit to raising up young leadership who will take significant leadership roles in reaching our city region.

> Now when Abram heard that his brother was taken captive, he armed his three hundred and eighteen trained

servants who were born in his own house, and went in pursuit as far as Dan (Gen. 14:14).

8. As a city Church, our desire is to be knit together as one corporate unified spiritual net making up the city Church, a network of covenantal relationships governed by covenantal relationships that will catch a great amount of fish—but the net won't break.

> Again, the kingdom of heaven is like a dragnet that was cast into the sea and gathered some of every kind (Matt. 13:47).

> Now I plead with you, brethren, by the name of our Lord Jesus Christ, that you all speak the same thing, and that there be no divisions among you, but that you be perfectly joined together in the same mind and in the same judgment (1 Cor. 1:10).

> From whom the whole body, joined and knit together by what every joint supplies, according to the effective working by which every part does its share, causes growth of the body for the edifying of itself in love (Eph. 4:16).

9. As a city Church, our desire is to turn the tide of wickedness to righteousness. We desire a full-blown, authentic revival to cover our city, resulting in new conversion growth in every Bible-believing, Jesus-centered church. We are believing that our prayers and presence will change the future of our city.

> Cry aloud, spare not; lift up your voice like a trumpet; tell My people their transgression, and the house of Jacob their sins (Isa. 58:1).

And I also say to you that you are Peter, and on this rock
I will build My church, and the gates of Hades shall not
prevail against it (Matt. 16:18).

Now then, we are ambassadors for Christ, as though God
were pleading through us: we implore you on Christ's
behalf, be reconciled to God (2 Cor. 5:20).

For we do not wrestle against flesh and blood, but
against principalities, against powers, against the rulers
of the darkness of this age, against spiritual hosts of
wickedness in the heavenly places (Eph. 6:12).

As a city Church consisting of many congregations and individuals, we have a great future if we will see the vision and work
God's plan. The challenge far exceeds our ability to meet the
needs, change the spiritual climate, and reach every house for
Christ. Yet, when the Holy Spirit is present with us and our
hearts are knit in the unity of such a goal, nothing is impossible.

Therefore if there is any consolation in Christ, if any
comfort of love, *if any fellowship of the Spirit,* if any affection and mercy, fulfill my joy by being like-minded, having the same love, being of one accord, of one mind. Let
nothing be done through selfish ambition or conceit,
but in lowliness of mind let each esteem others better
than himself. Let each of you look out not only for his
own interests, but also for the interests of others (Phil.
2:1-4, emphasis added).

Such city shaking begins with selflessness and prayer. This is
precisely why prayer intercession revival is happening all across

the globe. Intercession for our cities is the force that touches the heart and moves the hand to change the world. Our cities can and will be reached by a powerful Christ who is Lord over the city—as acknowledged by the leaders and congregants of those cities who will host the Holy Spirit through their united hearts and goals.

We can further that goal today by our united prayer:

Father, in the name of Jesus, let Thy kingdom come, let Thy will be done in our city. I stand with other leaders and believers in this city against the spirits that seek to destroy us. Together, we bind every spirit of rebellion, religious deception, blasphemy, immorality and witchcraft, and every spirit of destruction and division launched against us. Father God, release Your warring angels over our city. Release the Holy Spirit to do warfare against these enemies. Set this city free. Establish Your rule and reign in this city. Cause Your Holy Spirit to dwell within our borders—every household, every place. Cause revival fires to burn in Your church. Send revival to this city, in Jesus' mighty name, we pray. Amen!

Notes
1. Ted Haggard, *Primary Purpose* (Lake Mary, FL: Creation House, 1995), p. 76.
2. Ted Haggard and Jack W. Hayford, *Loving Your City into the Kingdom* (Ventura, CA: Regal Books, 1997), p. 14.
3. Haggard, *Primary Purpose*, p. 51.

Hosting the Holy Spirit Through

SERVING HUMANITY

by Bart Pierce

Bart Pierce is the pastor of Rock City Church in Baltimore, Maryland, where they have experienced the marvelous presence of God since January 1997. After this visitation of the Holy Spirit began, Rock Church was renamed to include the word "City." For years they have been actively involved in reaching the poor and needy of Baltimore, and they have sought to bring unity and a sense of purpose to the city Church as a whole. Recently, 85 pastors from churches all over Baltimore and from many denominations joined with Bart Pierce to sign an historic city covenant—a "declaration of dependence" upon one another to pray, to watchguard their city, to resolve conflicts in the spirit of reconciliation and to host the Lord together in their city. Bart has also written a book, Seeking Our Brothers *(Shippensburg, PA: Destiny Image, 2000).*

Shortly after I came to Baltimore in 1983, God spoke a word to me that would set the course of my own life and the purpose and vision of my church. When I first flew into Baltimore to begin my ministry, my heart's cry to God was, *Lord, give me my portion of this city.* Not many months later God spoke to me clearly: "If you'll take the ones nobody wants, I'll give you the ones everybody is after." I didn't know at the time the impact those words would have on my life, but our church has since been built on them.

Ever since I was born again during the Jesus Movement, my heart has gone out to the down-and-outer. Having come out of a life of drugs and crime myself, that's not so surprising. The church in Virginia Beach where I was saved opened their doors to whosoever, and hundreds of us flocked to that church in the early 1970s. It didn't seem to matter what we looked like or what stuff we'd been into; we were all welcome. So reaching out to the hurting became a part of my life and ministry from the beginning.

SERVING THE ONES NOBODY WANTS

Not long after we built our first sanctuary in Baltimore in 1983, the Rock Church's first outreach ministry got under way. No, there were no thundering words from God, just desperate people in need, which was enough to cause us to respond. Too many people today stand idly by, waiting for a voice from heaven or a prophetic word telling them God wants them to help people; but the heart of Jesus has always been to clothe the naked, feed the hungry, help the homeless and visit those in prison. At the Rock, we took His Word to mean precisely what it said and believed it to be for us today. We started *doing* what He said and from the very beginning, God began showing us what to do to effect change in our city.

Just as in the early days of my conversion, when hippies, gang members and druggies came in droves to that church in Virginia Beach, the same started coming into our church in Baltimore. Before long nearly our entire staff was made up of ex-druggies, prostitutes, thieves and the like. God's transforming power—combined with a little love, acceptance and a place to go—had turned these former losers into overcomers for the kingdom of God. In turn, they reached out to others who were needy.

We opened a home for unwed mothers first, primarily because I had grown tired of picketing abortion clinics without offering these girls a single tangible solution. We opened The Hiding Place in 1986. Since then we have assisted more than 500 girls in need, and more than 250 babies have been born at the house.

From there we started feeding the hungry. We began by having our church members bring a couple cans of food to the altar on Sunday mornings to help fill our food pantry. Today, we own a warehouse and three tractor trailers and distribute more than nine million pounds of food per year to soup kitchens, church pantries and hungry families. We call the ministry "A Can Can Make a Difference."

A shelter for men, Nehemiah House, was opened in 1991 to bring men in off the streets and give them a place to stay. Many of these men come to church to find Jesus and get filled with the love of God. Today, this 25-bed shelter (soon to be 50 beds!) is run by men from our church but is totally funded by grants from the government and private foundations in our county. So far we have received more than $2 million for the operation of Nehemiah House. The government is paying for sinners to come to our church to get saved! I'm not very smart, but if you ask me, I'd say that's a pretty good plan.

And why not? More than 2800 men have come to Nehemiah House, and the shelter has had a 72 percent success rate in taking homeless drug addicts off the street and seeing their lives completely changed. We now have a full-time church staff member whose sole job it is to write grants.

In 1987, the Rock Church started holding block parties on the worst streets of the inner city. We took musicians, clowns, puppets and a crew of servants who knew how to work and we fed, clothed and ministered to hundreds who poured into the streets of crime-ridden neighborhoods. We gave away bags of food, clothing and hot dogs to whomever would come. Hundreds and hundreds have been saved at the block parties over the years, and we give the names of those saved to the local churches. It wasn't uncommon for an inner-city church to have close to a hundred new folks in attendance on a Sunday morning following one of our block parties.

Little by little other churches started joining up with us to host these events; more than 40 blocks have been taken back from the enemy since 1987. Our burden and desire is to see all of Baltimore taken back for God—one block at a time.

HUNGRY FOR MORE

"If you'll take the ones nobody wants, I'll give you the ones everybody is after." I didn't have a clue back then what God really meant. Maybe I still don't fully understand it; but what began to happen when we answered His call was phenomenal. Doctors, lawyers, professional athletes and teachers began to come to our church. More awesome than that, these prosperous people caught the vision of the church and joined us in feeding, clothing and reaching out to the inner-city population.

Little did we know that there was even more—a lot more—that God wanted to do in the midst of this faithful congregation. Sure, we faced our ups and downs like any other church. The projects we had taken on were not always a "piece of cake"; they required a lot of hard work—blood, sweat and tears were a part of the process. But overall, things were good. People were getting saved, lives were being transformed, and our ministries were clicking along. Then, shortly after we moved into a new 3,000-seat sanctuary in 1995, God began to stir something within me.

I began to experience a kind of holy dissatisfaction. I found myself becoming sick of playing church and doing the same old, same old thing. Desperate for the reality of God, I began to cry out, "God, there's got to be more!" I was tired of sermons, songs and seminars. I wanted an encounter with the *living* God. I didn't want to hear somebody else's story or read about it in a book. Like Moses and like Jacob, I was ready to wrestle with Him until I could get ahold of Him, and I refused to go any farther unless He would go with me.

You might say that until that time I was like the blind man whom Jesus met outside the Temple. Jesus spat in the dirt and made mud with His saliva. He then rubbed the mud in the young man's eyes and healed him. After he was healed, people asked the man who this Jesus was that He could make the blind see. The young man said he didn't know anything about Jesus; all he knew was that once he was blind but now he could see (see John 9:1-25).

Having been shot at and wanted by the police, having once had a contract put out on my life and being in and out of jails, I have since lived 25 years being 100 percent on fire for God. Backsliding isn't a part of my vocabulary; it was never an option for me. You see, I know what it is like for God to touch me. He touched me, delivered me and saved me back in 1972. But after 25 years, there came a gnawing hunger within me for more. I had read about, studied and taught on revival for years, but I wanted to experience it.

God not only heard my prayer but He answered it. In January 1997, my wife and I went to an annual church fellowship retreat in Florida. There the power and presence of God came upon my life in a way I had never known. For days I could barely function because of the weight of the glory of God that covered me.

That weekend, Tommy Tenney, my wife and I spent hours talking about the glory of God and how we shared a common hunger for more of Him. I invited Tommy to travel with us to Baltimore and minister that weekend at our church. Tommy and I had been friends for some time, and he had shared with me about the church in Houston where he had been ministering when the glory of God came one Sunday morning and split the pulpit right down the middle. We talked about God for 18 hours as we drove home. Our hunger for Him was insatiable.

That Sunday morning God showed up in our church in an unprecedented way. Even before services started He was there. When we opened the doors of the church, people were all over the floor, weeping and crying out to God. We could barely get up to speak that morning because of His incredible presence in the room. We remained at church until the wee hours of the next morning and then came back Monday night for a prayer meeting that turned into another "glory meeting." We called another one for Tuesday, then the next week and the next. God just kept coming, manifesting His presence more and more strongly.

People began coming from everywhere, without any advertising of this event. We continued for months where we could barely function under the awesome presence of God. We wept, repented and cried out for forgiveness for having had church without Him for so long. We repented for doing things our way and for coming to be entertained instead of coming to entertain Him. We repented on behalf of our city, for the pastors and the churches in our city, for our nation, for our lack of worship and for pursuing our own agenda. We were tired of seeking His hand and what He could do for us; we just began to want Him and His face.

Sometimes, in the middle of the day people would come in, get caught up in the glory and find themselves in the building for hours, lying before Him and unable to move. Pastors from other churches came in and stayed longer than we did. They would thank us for letting them use our floor.

When God came into our church, His glory came into our church; and when His glory shows up, man can't stand in it. Things I had wanted to do since the beginning of my ministry have happened overnight. The miraculous has begun to happen. People are coming alive again! Healings are taking place, pastors are coming together, pulpits are being shared and the unity that is taking place among the Baltimore churches is phenomenal.

SERVING HIS HUMANITY, MINISTERING TO HIS DIVINITY

Several months into this outpouring, God began to speak to us about Mary and Martha. Now, after 14 years of reaching out to the poor in Baltimore, we knew about Martha, just as we knew about His hand of blessing and provision. But what God began to do—and what I sense has begun to happen all across the Body of Christ—concerns this simple principle derived from the biblical story of Mary and Martha.

When in Judea, the house Jesus went to more than any other was a house in Bethany where Mary and Martha and their brother, Lazarus, lived. Something drew Him there. Martha was the one who ministered to the humanity of Christ. And like Martha, I knew about the humanity of Christ and I knew the touch of God.

Just like that young blind man whom Jesus had healed, Jesus came and tapped me on the shoulder and turned me around one day and said, "Son, I'm the One who touched you." That was the beginning of my understanding of ministering to His divinity. His hand represents what He does for us—the serving part, the

Martha part, the anointing. His face represents His presence—who He is, the Mary part, His glory.

Understanding in this area is needed by the Church today, because there's a big difference between the anointing and the glory. I am so sorry that pastors and preachers have taken the anointing and smeared it all over themselves so that they would look and smell good to one another instead of using it for getting into His presence. He allows us to have His anointing so we can enter into His presence; but instead, we have pumped it and sprayed it so we can display something to others that we can do. The fact is, we can't do anything if He doesn't show up.

For far too long we have learned to have church without Him. We've learned to sing songs until we sing right through the back of the tabernacle and pass right by the Ark on the way out. We don't even know where He is most of the time. We come to church wanting something to happen. But we don't want it to happen under His conditions; we want it to happen under ours. I came to a place where I was sick of church. I began to cry out and said, "Oh God, I want You and Your agenda, not mine!"

It was time to get back to some of the basics at the church. During the first few months of revival when we could barely function, we had kept the ministries of the church going; but it was more like they were just barely functioning, too. I knew we had to get back into *working* them, but this presented somewhat of a conflict within us. On the one hand, we wanted to come in and lie before Him and do nothing but worship; on the other hand, God had called us to serve. Combining the two was the challenge.

Jesus liked going to Mary and Martha's home more than anywhere else in Judea. Why? Because they made Him feel welcomed. He was not only served there, but He was also ministered to. Martha served the humanity of Christ, while Mary ministered to the divinity of Christ. And if we can ever learn how to do both, we just might get all our dead brothers to come alive in the city!

What has been happening is that we've had "Martha churches" and "Mary churches." But God went to their house in Bethany and *both* of them were there. Some of us want to serve humanity, and some of us want to serve divinity. God wants these two parts of the Church to come together.

When we got up off the floor after lying in His presence for hours, there were still hungry, hurting people outside who knew nothing of what was happening within our four walls. While it was really comfortable inside, we had to learn to get up from that place, shake ourselves and go out there to minister to the whomsoever. We probably lost a few on the way out the door; but we also lost a few when He came in. Things like that just can't become your focus.

We became determined to see the glory of God touch those outside our church building as powerfully as those on the inside. So we continued

WE WERE DETERMINED TO SEE THE GLORY OF GOD TOUCH THOSE OUTSIDE OUR CHURCH BUILDING AS POWERFULLY AS THOSE ON THE INSIDE.

with the block parties, feeding the hungry and housing the homeless. And an amazing thing has happened. Not only have we seen those outside of the church getting touched, but we have seen more salvations within the church than ever! And the more we take Him out of the building, the more He comes in. The presence of God just gets heavier and heavier as the months go by. Our hearts are given to worshiping Him, because we know that true worshipers are the one thing He seeks after on this earth (see John 4:23).

I have asked myself, *Could it be that by taking care of the ones nobody wanted we would get God Himself to show up?* I had never considered this before. But after all, who *is* the One that everybody is after? The professionals? The rich? The upper class? No, it's God we want! And God is who we got.

As we go forth and host our fellow man, the Lord gives us every opportunity to host Him. We are called to feed the poor and hungry, clothe the naked, care for the sick and visit those in jail. Does it not say, "Whatever you did for one of the least of these brothers of mine, you did for me" (Matt. 25:40, *NIV*)? So in Baltimore we took Him at His Word and carried on where He left off. We were compelled to do these things and in the doing of them, we began to see Him in ways that are indescribable. Dead brothers came back to life. Churches were revived. The people were breathed on. Preachers rekindled their first love. Hearts across the city beat with passion for Him. Life!

We are not called to be doers of the Word only; we are also called to be worshipers. What we have found to be at the very heart of Jesus is the combining of the two. Why not? We can do both. We can be worshipers like Mary, sitting at His feet, listening and lavishing our love on Him. But I believe that Jesus also got hungry and tired, and Martha knew how to minister to His humanity and make Him feel comfortable. And He appreciated it. That's why He kept going back. Read it for yourself in the Gospels. He visited their home more than anyone else's. And when their brother, Lazarus, died, Jesus raised him from the dead.

Thousands of people have come to our church these past few years, and many of them have come, not only to worship with us, but also to inquire about our social ministries—our ministries of compassion. It's not uncommon for us to be found sprawled out on the floor, worshiping Him at night, and then doing daytime workshops on how to reach our cities. Many stay over to participate in block parties or to visit The Hiding Place and Nehemiah House and the food warehouse.

Our heart is simply to host the Holy Spirit, and as we learn to minister to Him, then maybe, just maybe, revival will come to our city and every dead thing will come alive. I believe this is the heart of God for every church in every city of the world. There's work to be done, and there's a God to be worshiped. And there's a revival waiting to happen.

A REVERENCE FOR THE PROPHETIC

by Cindy Jacobs

No one has spoken more life-changing prophetic words into my life than my friend Cindy Jacobs. She is founder and president of Generals of Intercession, an international ministry that works to help build prayer movements in nations around the world. Widely acknowledged as a prophetic voice to the Church, Cindy is the author of Women of Destiny *and* Possessing the Gates of the Enemy. *To learn more about how prophecy should work in the life of a local church, read her outstanding book on prophecy,* The Voice of God *(Ventura, CA: Regal Books, 1995).*

Do not quench the Spirit. Do not despise prophecies.
1 THESSALONIANS 5:19,20

For the testimony of Jesus is the spirit of prophecy.
REVELATION 19:10

The Holy Spirit is at home and present in the spirit of prophecy. Yet no other gift of the Spirit has proven more controversial in our churches than the gift of prophecy. In the contemporary

Church, the prophetic gift has often been misused, underrated, overrated—and yet it has brought immense blessing to the Body as well. The proper use of this valuable gift is necessary if the Church is to stay on the cutting edge of what God is doing. Why? Because it keeps us from falling into religious ruts or becoming institutionalized: in a word, boring.

The prophetic gift keeps the fresh wind of the Holy Spirit blowing across our congregations. There is nothing quite like receiving a word from God that confirms our secret desires, things we have uttered only in the private places of our hearts. I'm not saying that the Holy Spirit may not move in other ways without uttering a prophetic word. However, because the Bible says prophecy is a gift we should most earnestly desire (see 1 Cor. 14:39), we need to find a way to release it in our congregations.

A startling example of this was reported to me recently by a pastor friend. I have to tell you that when I heard it, my first thought was, *Did I prophesy that under the unction of the Holy Spirit?* A woman had come to the pastor and shared that when I prayed over her at a recent meeting a strange prophetic word came out of my mouth for her husband that went something like this: "You must tell your husband to go to the emergency room now! His life is in danger." The woman was, I'm sure, shaken by this word. It came at a time when her husband was traveling in another city. However, she believed that it was from God, so she called her husband and insisted that he go to the emergency room right away. Her husband, a bit perplexed by this unusual request, told her that he had been feeling a little ill but not enough to go to the hospital. The wife finally convinced him to go to the emergency room to be checked out. What he found out was astonishing! It seems he was bleeding internally and would have died within hours had he not gone to the hospital to be examined.

While not all prophecies produce such dramatic results, this is startling evidence that we need to learn to discern whether a prophecy given to us is from God and to act on it promptly if necessary.

Sadly, many churches that declare they believe in the gift of prophecy rarely see it moving in their congregations. Although they say that their theology makes room for and even embraces this gift, it is noticeably absent in the corporate meetings of the church. These same churches would claim that they follow the Bible and love the Word of God. Yet in practice it seems they are not doing what the Bible says:

> Pursue love, and desire spiritual gifts, but especially that you may prophesy (1 Cor. 14:1).

No other gift is spoken of by the Bible with such emphasis.

KNOWING THE PERFECT WILL OF GOD

The prophetic gift can give the direction, hope, balance and peace that many in the Body of Christ are seeking today. A word from the Lord can keep us from making decisions that may seem good but are not the perfect will of God for our lives.

One day I couldn't get my good friend Ché Ahn off my heart. At first I simply prayed for him, thinking that what I was feeling was the Spirit prompting me to intercede on his behalf. However, the burden continued to increase, and I knew then that this was a prophetic burden from the Lord and I needed to find him.

I hadn't talked to Ché for a while and didn't really know much of what was going on in his life. I also didn't have his home phone number, so I had to do some homework to find it. After a time I was able to connect with him, and he shared with me that he was seriously considering joining with a certain apostolic movement. The movement was a wonderful one that, personally, I loved. All of a sudden the Holy Spirit started to speak to me, telling me that Ché was *not* to join the new apostolic movement that was forming because he was going to be the head of a whole movement himself. Ché sounded a little surprised; but as he started to think, he realized that there were already beginning signs that other churches and pastors had a desire to align with the work he was doing at Harvest Rock Church in Pasadena, California.

Ché felt that this word was from the Lord and followed it by staying in relationship with the new apostolic movement but not aligning with it as an official member. Ché has since founded his own apostolic ministry, Harvest International Ministries, with (as of this writing) 161 churches in the United States and around the world.

CONFIRMING VISION

I personally believe that God assigns someone with a gift of prophecy to each and every church. The person may not be received or even fully understand that he or she is flowing in the prophetic. At times such persons may scare a pastor with some supernatural knowledge or wisdom. At times we may scare ourselves if we don't understand why we know what we know.

Nevertheless, the role of the prophetic is essential in confirming vision, especially at the local level. Once I was ministering at Word of Grace, a church in Mesa, Arizona, pastored by my good friend Gary Kinnaman. I looked out the side door of the church building and pointed at a street full of houses and apartment buildings. "Gary," I said, "There will be a day when you own that whole block, and you will build your new facility there."

And that is exactly what happened.

Word of Grace eventually purchased every house and apartment building and tore them down to make room for a beautiful new worship center that seats 2,000 people. And because the church acquired all the properties on either side of the street—about 20—the city of Mesa gave them at no cost a quarter-mile-long cul-de-sac bordering the north side of the campus!

What does this kind of prophetic word accomplish? Well, it gives us faith to believe for big things for a church. It reinforces vision and certainly fulfills the three uses of the prophetic, which are edification, exhortation and comfort (see 1 Cor. 14:3).

SPEAKING TO THE CITY

The following events surrounding the Columbine tragedy were first reported in the September/October 1999 issue of G.I. News, a bimonthly publication of Generals of Intercession.

The prophetic is not only vital to the spiritual health of a local church; it is also important if the Church is to understand and effect change to the spiritual climate of an entire city. In April 1999, a pastor's group from Denver asked me to come and share with them what God was saying for their city. The Denver area has a rich spiritual history; Kathryn Kuhlman and other ministers of the gospel have flowed in the miraculous there. Part of the prophetic word I gave that day pertained to the city's being a place of revival and miracles. The presence of the Lord was so strong at the meeting that many were visibly touched.

All of a sudden, the prophecy changed, and the Holy Spirit began to speak to us an unusual warning: "America will pay for its godlessness with the lives of its children." The prophecy then called for every city and suburb in the Denver region to establish a 24-hour prayer watch.

The pastors took the prophetic word seriously; they received the word and did not reject what was said. Unfortunately, none of them realized that the Lord meant *right now*.

A few days later, tragedy struck in the Denver suburb of Littleton. Littleton, Colorado, is an upper-middle-class city where everything looks peaceful and in order. No one expected what transpired in that lovely little city on April 20, 1999. That day, a pair of students dressed in black trench coats walked into Columbine High School and laid siege to their school, killing 13 classmates and a teacher and injuring at least 23 others. Like my friend Linda Mintle says, "Kids were killing kids." (Linda has written an excellent book on this topic that is published by Creation House.[1])

As I watched the news reports on television, I felt like someone had hit me in the stomach. Tears poured down my face as I remembered the words I had prophesied concerning our nation's children less than three weeks earlier. During the next few days I wondered, *Did God try to warn us in other ways?*

Now, I earnestly believe that the Christian young people who were killed—I've been told that eight of them were Christians—were martyrs for the Lord, Jesus Christ. I also realize that we have to deal with issues of the sovereignty of God. But I must ask the question: Could this have been avoided if we had heard His warnings and prayed? If so, what a painful lesson for us intercessors to learn!

This horrible event has spurred me to write and preach and do everything I can to stir up the gift of prophecy and prophetic intercession in the Body of Christ. If we ever needed to hear God speaking to us, the time is now. The very lives of our children may depend upon it!

Multiple Warnings

As it turned out, I wasn't the only one who received some type of warning before the shooting. A dream had been given to Bruce Porter, the pastor of one of the martyred teens, on January 20, 1999—exactly three months before the Columbine shooting:

> I awoke gasping for air, deep guttural cries escaping my lips. As I tried to collect my thoughts and calm my racing heart, I began to relate to my wife, Claudia, what I had just seen. "They were killing—no, slaughtering young people!" I blurted out. "Some of the kids were killing themselves! I could still see in my mind's eye the terrified faces of young men and women, boys and girls, bloody and crying. I could yet hear the sound of gunfire and what seemed to be muffled explosions. It seemed horrible! So real! As she coached me to remember, I cried and began to blurt out details of what I had just seen.
>
> I was in some sort of building. All around me were young people, and although I didn't realize it until now, they were obviously in a school setting. Suddenly they became bloody, and began to cry, scream and run in all directions. I saw what looked like red fire following behind them as they ran, and several fell down. I heard loud explosions and what sounded like firecrackers. Then the scene changed, and I saw some of these young

people running in a peculiar way. They were running in a line, holding their heads in their hands, crying, screaming, praying. . . . Some had blood on their faces, hands and torsos. The horror of that scene was palpable, and I felt their fear and anguish.

Then, as I watched, some of the young people began to change. They appeared as before, but their eyes changed and what seemed to be a look of determined certainty and confidence came over their faces. It was as if they had remembered something they had forgotten, something that took away their former terror and replaced it with a steely-eyed focus. I watched them turn around and go back into the place they came from. This time, however, these youths began to give aid to those who had fallen, some giving CPR, others binding wounds, praying and speaking things that seemed to enter into those listening to them like a vapor of some sort. There yet remained conflict, and I could see some of the red flame, but it seemed that a battle had been engaged and the young people were now winning. The words came to me . . . *Rescue 911.*[2]

This prophetic dream proved incredibly accurate as to the events that took place during the shooting. The two young men who did the killing had planted bombs throughout the school, and their gunshots sounded like firecrackers—only they were much more lethal.

A third warning was given to a prayer group led by Cheryl Morrison of Faith Bible Chapel in Arvada, Colorado, another Denver suburb. Susan Mendez of Denver's Channel 41 told me the details: One of the members of the prayer group had a vision the morning of the shooting during their regular 5:30 A.M.

prayer meeting. In her vision, she saw two men in black trench coats. She understood they were evil and, together with the other women in the group, prayed against the spirit of witchcraft. These prayers may have helped prevent the shooters from setting off their bombs before committing suicide.

Voices Crying in the Wilderness

This string of events has led me to ask other serious questions like, Would the two young men who perpetrated this act be alive today if more prayer had been raised up for their generation?

Given the volatility of the world we live in, it is vitally important that we not reject the legitimate words of the Lord given through our modern-day prophets. We need to heed these voices crying in the wilderness, because they are preparing the way of the Lord, preparing us for revival and a great harvest of souls.

The prophets are now loudly proclaiming to America and the nations of the earth that the time for repentance is at hand—that this is a time for purity and holiness. Our children are suffering because of our years of depravity and lack of absolutes. Relativism is eating us alive and producing extreme anger in the very children our forefathers fought to protect.

Scripture tells us that God will not do anything without first telling His prophets (see Amos 3:7). We are also promised in 2 Chronicles 20:20 that we will prosper if we listen to the prophets of God and believe them.

A group of 17 prophets gathered at the World Prayer Center in Colorado Springs on January 7, 1999. One respected prophet gave a word to some of the prophets who were there that the walls were down in Colorado Springs and that, in case of terrorism, we would be the first hit. Those of us who heard that word believed it. This wasn't an entirely new thought to us. God had already been speaking to us about the pride of our city. We knew our walls were down.

How did we respond to that word? First of all, we acknowledged it to be true. We then met with a group of city church leaders and began to devise a strategy to rebuild the walls of protection over our city immediately. As we met, we formed a strategy to implement a time of 40 days of 24-hour praise and prayer. As praise ascended day and night in homes all across the city, a dozen corporate gatherings were held in the World Prayer Center, led by various worship teams from the city.

WE NEED TO HEED THESE VOICES CRYING IN THE WILDERNESS, BECAUSE THEY ARE PREPARING THE WAY OF THE LORD.

Other strategies we used during this 40 days included reading from the Bible at a hundred troubled locations throughout the city. Sites of known occult practices, high schools, colleges and military bases were among the places visited. Stakes with Scripture verses placed on them were driven into the ground at these locations as prophetic acts.

Our 40 days of praise ended with a Jesus march organized by Ken and Solveig Henderson of Soldiers for Jesus. The icing on the cake was when we partnered with Operation Blessing under the mandate of Isaiah 58 to feed the poor in the city.

What did these actions actually accomplish to protect our city? One indication came in a surprising revelation given to me by an intercessor in Denver, Colorado. I talked with her while on stage at the Denver Coliseum on the Saturday night following the Columbine incident. This lovely lady came up and showed me a map of the school shootings that had taken place in America in recent years. What I saw was amazing indeed! They were all on two straight lines. One line ended in Waco, Texas, where some 90 people had been killed in the now-infamous standoff between the FBI and a religious cult in the spring of 1993.[3] The second line stopped in Oklahoma City, where 168 men, women and children had died when a massive bomb destroyed the Murrah Federal Building in April 1995.[4]

As I studied the map I realized that one city along the straight line had been spared: Colorado Springs. Could it be that the walls of praise, raised by the citywide church of Colorado Springs, had protected our city? I believe so. I am told that a young man in Colorado Springs turned himself in to his high school counselor one week after the Columbine incident. His statement? "I need help. . . . I was going to do the same thing that happened at Columbine High."

DO YOU HEAR WHAT I HEAR?

It seems to me that God is trying to warn us of impending judgments. He wants to alert individual churches, as well as cities and nations. He is a God of mercy and grace; but He is also a God who judges sin.

Critics who attack the modern prophetic movement fail to understand that Satan is furious that the alarm is being sounded by God's prophetic people. Does there need to be balance and accountability in the prophetic movement? Of course! The prophets I know welcome and believe in these two things.

One way we can better utilize what God is saying through His people is to "harvest" the prophetic intercessors. After hearing the prophecies that were given to us here in Colorado, I knew we had not been able to hear what God was saying in all its fullness. We were as watchmen scattered along the wall, not communicating what we were seeing from our various posts. This is the case in most churches and cities. We have a hearing loss in our cities because the Body of Christ is not properly aligned. Those with prophetic gifts are scattered and isolated from each other and from the rest of the Body of Christ.

Here are a few suggestions to help restore our sensitivity of hearing:

- Pastors and local church leaders, you need to know and recognize the prophetic voices in your local congregation. Meet with these prophetic people to hear or confirm what God is saying to your local expression of the Body of Christ.
- Recognize and gather the proven prophetic intercessors in your city.
- Appoint a group of pastors and leaders as a *prophetic filter* to judge and disseminate what your intercessors are hearing from God.
- Set up an e-mail address with a password by which these two groups can enter any prophetic words they are receiving from the Lord. What if the Denver area had had such an e-mail site and Bruce Porter's dream had been posted for prayer? What if someone else had read the word the Lord gave through me and put it together with the intercessor's vision of the men in black trench coats? This could have resulted in a powerful, focused time of intercessory prayer that may have warded off disaster.
- If a prophetic word is giving a warning of a crisis or judgment, ask the Lord how to pray over the word. Is

there a specific time frame for the fulfillment of the word? (For example, in the case of an impending natural disaster, when is it to take place?) Are there any conditions given in the word? It might be that the judgment can be averted if repentance is made for a certain sin (e.g., idolatry).

God wants us, as the Church, to grow in the prophetic. I've watched the worldwide prayer movement grow from a small effort in 1989 to one that C. Peter Wagner now says is "totally out of control"—there is no stopping it! Could this happen with our ability to hear the voice of God concerning our cities during the next decade?

We are living at a *kairos* moment, a strategic time when God wants to visit cities and nations with revival. There is a revival in the birth canal just waiting to be born! The Church needs the prophetic to help push the baby out of its dark place and birth an explosion of the miraculous, a wondrous harvest of souls and deep moves of repentance throughout the Church. Meanwhile, Satan is working feverishly to sow discouragement in the hearts of believers so they don't have the strength to push through in prayer for the birth of this revival (see Isa. 37:3). The prophetic word will clue us in to the enemy's hindrances that stand in the way of the birth.

A group of intercessors here in Colorado Springs had a vision that the city was very pregnant but its womb was sutured shut with the sin of the city. So they sought the Lord in prayer and studied the past sins of Colorado Springs to remove these hindrances to the powerful move of the Holy Spirit that God has promised us through His prophets.

The Lord is doing a new thing across the nations of the earth. This move of God will not be like the last. He is shaking our cities and nations. There has probably never been a day like the one we live in at the dawn of this new millennium. We need to hear what God is saying now. Thousands are in darkness, waiting for His voice to speak into their hearts the Word of God that will bring them into the glorious light of the gospel. Let us obey the biblical admonition to earnestly desire to prophesy. Let us loose and release the prophetic gift within our churches, cities and nations. Thus we will allow His glorious voice to be heard and revival to be born.

Notes

1. Linda Mintle, *Kids Killing Kids* (Lake Mary, FL: Creation House, 1999).
2. Bruce Porter, quoted in "Heeding the Word of the Prophets," *G.I. News* (September/October 1999).
3. "Six Years Later, Waco's Horror Is Still Hazy," *CNN.com*, September 25, 1999. http://www.cnn.com/US/9909/25/wacos.dark.questions (accessed April 24, 2000).
4. "Oklahoma City Tragedy: The Bombing," *CNN Interactive*, 1996. http://www.cnn.com/US/OKC/bombing.html (accessed April 24, 2000).

HOSTING GUEST MINISTRIES

by Wendell Smith

When we think of hosting the Holy Spirit, we often imagine it as some intangible way of creating an atmosphere in the Spirit that would cause Him to be drawn and remain. We know that the character of the Holy Ghost is that of a gentleman—never pushing, but respectful, considerate and gentle. Yet one of the most easily overlooked ways of hosting the Holy Spirit is to graciously and generously embrace those whom God sends our way, be they leaders in the Body of Christ, strangers, orphans, widows or even the smallest child. Wendell and Gini Smith are dear friends and are the pastors of City Church in Kirkland, Washington, a suburb of Seattle. I know of no one who does a better job of wooing the Holy Spirit by honoring those whom God sends their way.

He who receives you receives Me, and he who receives Me receives Him who sent Me.

MATTHEW 10:40

I remember being an impressionable teenager when my father brought a particularly odd-looking stranger to our house. We had never seen anyone like him before, and he had the appearance of a man we had no desire to see again. I saw my mother gulp and roll her eyes as Dad introduced him to the family. Dad, as always, was driven by compassion for the destitute, with which Mom would eventually cooperate, and we knew that God would watch over us, so everything would, as usual, turn out right.

The small man was dressed very shabbily, and he smelled as bad as he looked, which only supported my negative and somewhat fearful attitude. The first thing Dad did was to get him into a hot bath; I can't remember what we did with his clothes, but they disappeared. Dad, the miracle worker, scrounged up some clothing that the man could hang on his bony body.

After taking a bath and donning the fresh clothing, our visitor spent an hour or so talking with us around the kitchen table, while Mom prepared and served him a hot meal. After some interesting conversation and a prayer from Dad, the man went on his way, walking away from our house, waving, with a big smile on his face and a thankful glance back. Watching him slowly disappear into the distance, my imagination ran wild conjuring up images of who this mystery man might be. My fantasies prompted me to question my father's judgment in taking a chance bringing a man like that into our house. I have never forgotten my father's response—my first introduction to this subject in Scripture. He leaned toward me with that look in his eyes that said, *This is something you need to know*. Then my father quoted from the book of Hebrews: "Don't forget to entertain strangers, because some have entertained angels unawares" (see Heb. 13:2).

My three brothers and I were mesmerized at the thought that this stranger could have been an angel. We contemplated the idea late into the night, trying to remember the man's every expression and mannerism that we might verify a possible celestial visitation to our humble home. Had we just been visited and evaluated by a heavenly being? Or was he just an unfortunate man in need of our practical expression of love and kindness? Either way, my Dad was the hero, and we were his students that night, a lesson from Hospitality 101 now imbedded in our memory banks for future reference.

A TANGIBLE DEMONSTRATION OF FAITH AND LOVE

During the late 1980s and early 1990s, my family traveled across America with the youth seminar Dragonslayer. We were invited to a diverse selection of churches, including many different denominations, geographical settings and congregational sizes. Once we were invited to one of America's largest churches to present the three-day Dragonslayer seminar. At the close of a profitable program, we were preparing to leave less-than-desirable accommodations when we were given an envelope which we assumed contained a check to cover our honorarium and traveling expenses. We opened that envelope to find that, much to our dismay, the church had paid only half our expenses and had given us a minimal honorarium. The total did not even meet our travel costs! Normally, a salaried resident pastor could swallow hard and go on, but this was our only means of livelihood. We had children to feed, a staff back home to support and a full-time ministry traveling from one city to the next. This insufficient check was not going to get us very far.

When we returned home, I asked my senior pastor's counsel, and he wisely instructed us to trust the Lord in these matters. He related similar instances from his ministry travels and encouraged us that this was a good test of our motives for ministry. He also challenged us to believe the Lord to make it up to us.

The next week we were scheduled for a meeting in Cleveland,

Ohio, at Pastor Ken Roberts' church, which was associated with People of Destiny and my friend Larry Tomczak. I mention their names here because their generosity led to a hallmark experience that my family would treasure and remember. At the conclusion of the three-day seminar, the pastor graciously requested that the participants give generously in a love offering to be taken on behalf of our ministry. Our previous experience still fresh in our thinking, we were concerned with the pastor's low-key appeal, especially since they had taken no other offerings for us. To add to our feelings of anxiety, it was a Saturday afternoon, and nearly a third of the 400 people attending had already left the rented school auditorium, and those who remained were primarily teenagers.

The pastor suggested that the ushers take up the offering, immediately count it and publicly announce the amount. I thought, *Oh no, don't do that and embarrass yourself.* When the amount of the offering was finally made public, I was privately embarrassed by my limited faith. "We have received $4,700 for the Smiths," the pastor announced, "and the elders have met and decided to match that amount because we believe in this ministry." We were overwhelmed by their tangible demonstration of faith and love! To this day, no one church has ever matched the nearly $10,000 given to our ministry on that occasion. I love to retell the story.

A PROPHET'S REWARD

He who receives a prophet in the name of a prophet shall receive a prophet's reward. And he who receives a righteous man in the name of a righteous man shall receive a righteous man's reward. And whoever gives one of these

little ones only a cup of cold water in the name of a disciple, assuredly, I say to you, he shall by no means lose his
reward (Matt. 10:41,42).

The passion and desire of every prophet is to have a vital sense of
the anointing of God's presence and power. To receive a
prophet's reward means to receive that same powerful anointing.

The rewards of a righteous man are the blessings of peace and
joy. The Bible says "a faithful man will abound with blessings"
and that the kingdom of God is "righteousness and peace and
joy" (Rom. 14:17). If you receive a righteous man, Jesus teaches
that you will receive His reward, which is a blessing of peace and
a blessing of joy.

The reward of a disciple is revelation. The passion of a follower is to learn from the Master and to receive wisdom and
understanding. Giving a cup of cold water to a little one qualifies
you to receive the disciple's reward.

The rewards of more anointing, joy and revelation will come
to you and your church when you receive prophets, righteous
people and little ones. Treating them as you would the Lord will
ensure His great reward.

How then should you receive an anointed minister? How
about a good man or a dedicated follower of the Lord? Would
you receive a minister from another denomination or doctrinal
stream? Would you receive a woman minister, a minister of
another race or a preacher who is young enough to be your son
or daughter or even your grandchild? Here's what the Word has
to say on the subject:

Therefore receive one another, just as Christ also received
us, to the glory of God (Rom. 15:7).

Hosting Guest Ministries   127

I commend to you Phoebe our sister, who is a servant of
the church in Cenchrea, that you may receive her in the
Lord in a manner worthy of the saints, and assist her in
whatever business she has need of you (Rom. 16:1,2).

Receive him therefore in the Lord with all gladness, and
hold such men in esteem; because for the work of Christ
he came close to death, not regarding his life (Phil.
2:29,30).

Also prepare a guest room for me, for I trust that through
your prayers I shall be granted to you (Philem. 22).

Do faithfully whatever you do for the brethren and for
strangers, who have borne witness of your love before the
church. If you send them forward on their journey in a
manner worthy of God, you will do well, because they
went forth for His name's sake. . . . We therefore ought to
receive such, that we may become fellow workers for the
truth (3 John 5-8).

Can you imagine hosting Jesus in your church? How would
you treat Him? What if the apostle Paul visited your congregation to make an apostolic adjustment or two? Would you be prepared to receive him, to treat him properly and to honor him in
his position of grace and authority?

The manner in which our congregations receive guest ministers and preachers of the gospel is indicative of the way they
receive the Lord and the ministry of the Holy Spirit. God chooses men and women to pour His Spirit upon, and He anoints
them to bless others. To the degree we value and esteem these
emissaries of the gospel, to that same degree will our churches

benefit and be edified. When we exercise faith in and respect for the ministers, their faith is released to impart the Word of God to our churches with greater confidence and without unnecessary distraction. Ministry is hindered when guest ministers are focused on their poor accommodations or their need for a hot shower or worse.

In our years of travel, we have been housed in some of the most unusual places: church basements with no access to running water; adorable children's bedrooms furnished only with bunk beds; budget hotels stocked with plentiful supplies of plastic cups and enhanced by the odor of cigarette smoke; vacated homes where we were awkwardly left to fend for ourselves in the midst of someone else's stuff; truck campers that were driven off with us still asleep inside (that will make your heart beat faster!); trailers located conveniently in the church parking lot; and the occasional cabin in the woods with outhouse access. While traveling we learned to adapt to a variety of conditions and to make do without complaint, but in these uncomfortable situations we inwardly questioned whether the pastor had respect for our ministry. The circumstances subtly undermined our assurance, rendering our ministry less effective by hindering our faith and boldness.

In the Old Testament we find many examples of kindness and hospitality shown to traveling "ministers." Abraham helped Sarah to prepare a meal for visiting angels (see Gen. 18:6). The woman of Shunem had a special chamber added to her house so that the prophet Elisha could stay with her and her family (see 2 Kings 4:8-10). The harlot Rahab lodged the spies of Israel and became part of the genealogy of Christ (see Josh. 2:1; Matt. 1:5).

The Gospel writers relate many stories of how Jesus was entertained in the homes of others. Mary and Martha and their brother, Lazarus, had the privilege of hosting the Lord (see Luke 10:38). Zacchaeus was chosen by Jesus to experience a divine appointment through which salvation came to his house (see Luke 19:5). Even Simon the leper received Jesus into his house (see Mark 14:3).

At the dawn of the Church era in the book of Acts, hospitality abounded as many church gatherings were held in homes. In key cities throughout Asia, churches were launched in homes where the residents believed on the Lord and received the apostles. The disciples were gathered in someone's upper room when the Holy Spirit first fell upon them. Just after his conversion, Saul stayed in the house of Judas on a street called Straight. Peter was staying at the house of Simon the Tanner by the sea when Cornelius sent for him, asking Peter to come to a house of spiritually hungry Gentiles. The Philippian jailer brought Paul and Silas from the prison to his house and received the glorious gospel.

The Acts of the Apostles ends with a story of the kindness of Publius, the leading citizen of a certain island, who courteously entertained Paul and his shipwrecked companions for three days (see Acts 28). Publius demonstrated unusual graciousness, welcoming them, warming them, entertaining them, honoring them and providing for them the things that were necessary for resuming their journey. As a result of his ministry of hospitality, many people on that island were healed of their diseases, making me wonder what other rewards came to those friendly island people who harbored and blessed the great apostle.

What a privilege for these new converts to host Jesus or the apostle Paul! Can you imagine the honor? And yet that is exactly what Jesus says we can know when we welcome and value those who come to us in His name:

Then the righteous will answer Him, saying, "Lord, when did we see You hungry and feed You, or thirsty and give

You drink? When did we see You a stranger and take You in, or naked and clothe You? Or when did we see You sick, or in prison, and come to You?" And the King will answer and say to them, "Assuredly, I say to you, inasmuch as you did it to one of the least of these My brethren, you did it to Me" (Matt 25:37-40).

For whoever gives you a cup of water to drink in My name, because you belong to Christ, assuredly, I say to you, he will by no means lose his reward (Mark 9:41).

Whoever receives this little child in My name receives Me; and whoever receives Me receives Him who sent Me (Luke 9:48).

HOW TO HOST A VISITING MINISTRY

After years of both traveling in ministry and receiving ministries into our church, we have learned some insightful keys to hosting guest ministries. Most importantly and very simply, first treat them with dignity and respect. Here are some practical dynamics that will help you successfully host visiting guest ministries and ensure the wonderful rewards that follow.

Communicate frequently and clearly with your invited guests and verify the plans, details and expectations of their time with you.

When inviting guest ministers who are unfamiliar with our church, we find it helpful to send them photos of our building, our people and some of our most anointed gatherings so our guests can visualize our church community. Communicate with your guests by letter, fax, e-mail and by phone to give them all the information they will need in order to know what is expected of them. Most speakers would appreciate a packet of information from your church, complete with photos, directions, vision materials, doctrinal statements and church background.

Before visiting churches as a guest ministry, we have had churches fax us a list of questions, requesting a list of our favorite foods, hobbies and recreational desires. When we arrived at those churches, we felt honored and blessed that they put so much effort into making us comfortable during our stay.

Make proper preparations for the arrival of guest ministers and your initial reception of them.

Unfortunately, my wife, our children and I have found ourselves at many an airport baggage-claim area, waiting to be picked up by an unknown church representative. Playing mind games to pass the time, we would try guessing what the person would look like and what had delayed them from rescuing us from the conveyor belts.

When a speaker arrives by air, have a congenial, positive person—preferably a pastor or key leader—pick him or her up at the airport gate. Your representative should dress smartly, park the vehicle (or leave it at the baggage area with another driver) and be prompt, at the gate waiting for the guest to deplane. The representative should greet the visiting minister with a smile and a warm handshake, ready to help carry bags and to guide your guest through the airport.

Guests should never have to wait or be left guessing who is picking them up, and they should never have to call the church to get a ride. The host-church representative should be able to make pleasant conversation and be ready to answer basic questions concerning the church, its history, its ministries, your city and the community. The driver should obey all traffic laws, including the speed limit, and make sure the car is fueled up before going to the airport. The representative should present the guest minister with a meeting schedule, including all service times, prayer times, workshop times, appropriate attire for each event, meal times and menu, pickup times and drivers' names and phone numbers, the address and phone number of the accommodations, the contact person's name and phone number and any other pertinent information. The guest minister should be taken directly from the airport to his or her hotel, avoiding sightseeing tours or side trips to a hospital to pray with someone.

Reserve one of the best hotel rooms in the area for your guests.

Those of us who travel extensively have many horror stories about some of the places and homes where we have stayed. We have stayed on hide-a-beds in people's living rooms, used family restrooms with no locks on the doors, slept on dirty sheets and dodged cockroaches in the night. We have slept on rock-hard beds in budget motels and have had to clean our own rooms. Once our hotel registration was lost and when the pastor came to pick us up, the hotel claimed we were not registered!

Your guests should be pre-checked into the hotel, leaving a credit card imprint on file for all room charges. The room should exceed your guest's requests and include a basket of healthy snack foods and fruit and a greeting card or letter from the senior pastor. Allow them to make charges to their room and make arrangements to meet any immediate needs they might have, such as laundry or dry cleaning.

At times, there are situations where a spacious and comfortable home with guest facilities is available for accommodations, but this is rare and can often be awkward and distracting for a minister.

Provide first-class transportation for your guests.

When speaking for Pastor Sonny Argonzoni's church, Victory Outreach in La Puente, California, we were surprised and a little overwhelmed when he sent a limousine to transport us to the church. A church member owned a limousine service and provided the vehicle for the occasion free of charge. Although it was not necessary or expected, you can imagine how we felt, munching on delicious breakfast snacks on the way to church and stepping out of a beautiful limo to arrive at their anointed service. We were ready to minister and felt greatly honored.

The best scenario for transporting your guests in most situations is a relatively new and roomy automobile or a clean and easy-to-step-into van. I once had to chauffeur former NFL great Rosey Grier in a large van because nothing else would fit him comfortably.

Recently, much to our chagrin, we inadvertently left a guest speaker's wife at the hotel, where she was waiting for us to pick her up for the service. As much as you try to follow through on every detail when entertaining guests, sometimes details get missed; in this case it happened to a most beloved friend. The couple forgave us, and we learned to communicate better concerning details.

Some ministers may request a rental car; in these cases, exceed their request and provide a large, roomy, newer vehicle. Reservations and rental charges should be taken care of in advance by the host church. Be generous.

Limit the guests' ministry to the purpose of their visit.

We were ministering in a large church and, after an extended service, we were quite weary from pouring ourselves out in preaching and prophecy and prayer. The pastor guided us into a side room, where we expected to rest and regroup for the next session. As we sat down to rest, the pastor ushered into the room a couple from his church and asked us to counsel them. Not only were we tired and shocked, but under the circumstances I am not sure our counsel was all that helpful. The pastor had given us no advance warning or knowledge of the situation, and our counsel may very well have contradicted the pastor's own advice.

If you want the best from visiting ministers, don't ask them to solve all your church's problems during a short visit. Let them function in the area of their grace and fulfill the reason for which you invited them. Do not ask guest ministers to counsel your church members or to try to solve a long-standing church problem unless they are spiritually related to you or are functioning in an apostolic role over your church.

Pray for your guests before they minister.

In our travels, the only pastor who ever prayed with me extensively before a service was Fred Kropp, who pastored a growing church in Harrisonville, Missouri. Early on a Sunday morning in his office, we got down on our knees and prayed for more than an hour. He prayed over me and blessed me and released me to minister to his flock. I was very touched, and I never forgot his kindness. Today, he and his family are on staff with us in Seattle.

We are dependent on the intercessors who are assigned to pray for my wife, Gini, and me and who cover all our services in prayer. When guest ministers arrive, I have these chosen and anointed men and women pray for them. Nearly every speaker who has addressed our congregation has commented more positively about the intercessors' ministry than about any other ministry of our church.

A preacher who enters the gates of our church should be given the authority to minister and the freedom to exercise his or her gifts among our people. We pray this over guest speakers and release them to speak to the flock with all authority and boldness.

PRAY OVER GUEST SPEAKERS AND RELEASE THEM TO SPEAK TO YOUR FLOCK WITH ALL AUTHORITY AND BOLDNESS.

Discretion should be exercised when praying for a guest. The laying on of hands should be discreet; the prayers should be gentle and their duration not so long as to frustrate your guest or cause him or her to feel uncomfortable. I was receiving prayer in a church before a service when intercessors were unleashed upon me, laying their hands all over me, messing my hair, scuffing my shoes and wrinkling my suit coat. We want to welcome the Holy Spirit without disheveling the minister of the gospel. Do not be dissuaded, however. Guests need prayer and spiritual covering before they minister in your church.

Make appropriate arrangements to protect your guests during services.

When a gunman entered John Hagee's church and unloaded his pistol in the pastor's direction one Wednesday night, I am sure the ushers never expected it. When drug lords attempted to assassinate a great Colombian pastor in Bogota, no one was ready to defend him. We live in a dangerous world where people can be driven by devils to do most anything. Recent headlines tell stories of demonized people taking the lives of believers within the sanctuary of churches. This is not to say that you should hire armed bodyguards, but precautions for security and safety should be taken to care for guest ministers while they are in your church and your city.

At our church in Seattle we are blessed with the most competent ushers in the world. Our ushers take their ministry very seriously, and they view their ministerial position as significant to the success of the church. They train, practice and pray to be more proficient. An usher is assigned to both my wife and me at all times during our services. We also have qualified men and women overseeing the entire facility during our services. These men and women are able to communicate with each other by radio and, at a moment's notice, can alert each other of any potential problem or changes or additions to the meeting.

During special services, an usher should be assigned to your guest's side at all times. One of the responsibilities of this usher should be to shield him or her from possible unpleasant situations. The usher should also carry the guest's personal items, Bible and briefcase and be prepared to escort the guest all over the facility.

At the conclusion of a service, do not leave your guest waiting while you greet the saints and do your pastoral work for the week. At least have an usher or a qualified staff member take the guest to your private office, where he or she can rest and be refreshed.

Make proper introductions of the minister before your people.

I was once introduced to a church where I had never ministered before by a pastor who causally commented, "And now we're glad to have Wendell here," and then handed me the microphone. I was left to introduce myself. This can be embarrassing for a guest minister, having to explain who he is, why he is there and why he is qualified to speak to the lives of your people.

A host pastor should appear knowledgeable about the general details of a guest minister's background—titles, achievements, position—so as to provide an effective introduction. A formal, flowery introduction can be overkill in most cases; but a trite introduction that leaves the people without a clue as to who is addressing them can be much worse.

We not only give adequate and detailed introduction of our guest ministers, but we also often promote books or materials they have authored, introduce their spouse and children or other guests who may be traveling with them, and we sometimes show a brief video clip of their church or ministry. Our people always spontaneously stand and give a heartfelt ovation to a guest who has come to preach the Word of God to us.

Explain your expectations to the minister before services start.

Years ago I was asked to preach at a church where the senior pastor was very exact and demanding. He instructed me that I had precisely 29 minutes to speak. At the conclusion of my sermon, I handed the service back to him with 30 seconds to spare. He apparently liked the message and appreciated my timeliness, because he asked me to give an altar appeal, which I did. I was not bothered by the exactness of the pastor, nor was I offended by his time limitations. I felt secure knowing exactly what was expected of me.

Communicating your expectations will guard against misunderstandings and provide clear boundaries for ministry. Explain in advance, preferably in writing, what you expect of the minister, especially in regard to ministry to people. When he concludes his sermon, do you want him to give an altar call, turn the service back to you, dismiss the people or start a Jericho march? Let your guests know what you expect. Inform them of time constraints, being as generous as possible and giving them adequate time to speak to the people.

Ask your guests what kind of recreation they would enjoy while they are with you.

When we were traveling more frequently, we were often treated to daytime sight-seeing tours. In most cases, these cut into our study and prayer time for evening services, and I then did not feel adequately prepared or rested for ministry. Although we often enjoyed the beautiful scenery, sight-seeing was not the purpose for which I had been invited.

One or two speakers we have hosted in our church enjoyed playing racquetball, so we planned in advance to lodge them in a local hotel that was equipped with a health club and racquetball courts. Most speakers prefer during their free time to either rest or do some kind of light exercise. You can usually leave this to them.

A good host, however, should not just drop guests off after a service or leave them alone all day without knowing the guests' needs or desires. We have found that, during the daytime, most guests enjoy briefly seeing our city before having a nice, healthy meal at a restaurant with a variety of options and then getting back to their hotel room with plenty of time to rest, study and pray before an evening meeting.

Never force an activity on a guest speaker. Guests often prefer to make their own plans, and they may not be interested in your planned trip to a nearby mountain, with a two-hour hike up to the summit to pick the most beautiful purple flowers they have ever seen. Ask ahead of time to determine whether you ought to plan on joining them for a round of golf, launching a yacht, renting some bicycles or breaking out the chess board.

Pastors Mark and Nicole Conner of Waverly Christian Church in Melbourne, Australia, along with Mark's father, Kevin, are delightful hosts. They have personally taken us on unusual Australian excursions, while at the same time being sensitive to give us time to rest and pray before ministering. They are extremely generous and hospitable in their care for their guests.

Provide quality food for your guests during their stay.
Preaching in New Orleans, Louisiana, for Pastor Charles Green, we were honored and blessed when he and his lovely wife took us to lunch one afternoon. They were senior pastors of a large church who showed us great kindness, even though we were just youth pastors at the time. They treated us to an outstanding meal at one of their favorite restaurants, complete with catfish, hush puppies, greens and all the fixings.

Although home-cooked meals can be delightful, most speakers prefer a restaurant with a quiet atmosphere, some good fellowship and a nourishing meal. If you plan to provide a fellowship meal of some kind after a service, include a variety of healthy and nourishing foods. Do not serve your guests fast food. Also, honor your guests by allowing them to be served first.

And it is always a treat for your guests to arrive at their hotel room to find a basket of healthy snacks.

Be sensitive and discreet in showing hospitality to your guests.

I have memories of many late-night meetings in people's homes after services, where I tried to keep my eyes open while people asked us questions or relayed their latest vision. In most of these cases, the church would have been better served by allowing us to have a brief fellowship time and then get to bed. Most speakers do not want to spend long hours of fellowship at your leaders' homes; your hospitality can be a distraction from the reason you asked them to come to your church.

Be friendly and make it your goal to set your guests at ease and to make them feel welcomed and blessed. Encourage them and compliment them sincerely about their ministry. Communicate after the service as to how you thought they ministered, focusing on the positive things you appreciated. Most ministers appreciate sincere affirmation, and they usually welcome questions about their life and ministry. Be a good listener.

Dr. James Marocco of the First Assembly of God in Maui honors all special guests and ministers, even if they are just visiting while on vacation, with a personally hosted fellowship time in his private office area after services. He and his wife provide food and a quiet place to share and to get to know other ministers.

Honor guest ministers with generous honorariums, love offerings and expense reimbursements.

This is a very sensitive point with ministers who are trusting God to provide as they travel, giving their lives for people and helping to build the churches of other preachers. The Bible is clear in this area, and the Word plainly makes the point that ministers are honored or dishonored by how we treat them financially:

For if the Gentiles have been partakers of their spiritual things, their duty is also to minister to them in material things (Rom. 15:27).

Who ever goes to war at his own expense? Who plants a vineyard and does not eat of its fruit? Or who tends a flock and does not drink of the milk of the flock? If we have sown spiritual things for you, is it a great thing if we reap your material things? (1 Cor. 9:7,11).

When setting the amount of an honorarium, I recommend that pastors double the generous amount they have determined to give. Most pastors are far too conservative when honoring speakers, especially if they have never traveled themselves. We will reap what we sow.

The status of a preacher should also be taken into consideration. For example, if the speaker is from an apostolic ministry or receives his or her full livelihood from traveling and speaking engagements, that person should be given more and blessed liberally.

When a minister is leaving your church after a visit, when possible, have a check ready. Separate checks should be given for expenses (made out to the church or organization) and for honorarium (made out to the minister personally).

In special cases, an additional love offering for the guest's church or ministry may be given as well. Although it is acceptable to mail a check, it is best to put it in guests' hands when they leave. It has happened in unusual circumstances that I never did receive anything in the mail, and in one situation I received the check a full year later because the accounting office had forgotten to send it.

Consider using other creative ways to bless and to show love to guest ministers. We have often purchased gifts for guests or their family members as a token of special appreciation and love. In one instance my wife, Gini, took the four daughters of a guest pastor to the shopping mall and gave them each $100 cash and, just for fun, she challenged them to spend it all in one hour or they had to return it. Not only did the girls have a blast spending the money (none was returned), but our guests were deeply touched by my wife's generosity. If you want to truly bless a minister and his wife, do something special for their children.

Pastor Rick Benjamin in Anchorage, Alaska, once treated us to a plane ride over the glaciers. Another pastor gave us a small amount of cash to spend in any way we wanted while we were with him. Not only have I had the joy of being the recipient of many generous gifts, but I have also had the privilege of seeing the stunned faces and grateful hearts of missionaries and needy ministers when I bought them a suit or a briefcase or a computer.

In one case, I wanted to bless Pastor Steven Kaylor of Hope Church in Tokyo, Japan. Gini and I took him shopping for a watch, pretending to want it for ourselves. When we found a watch that he also liked, we purchased it and gave it to him. He was shocked and surprised at our kindness. Later, he was greatly embarrassed when we found out that the watch that we had thought cost $150 actually cost $1,500. We told him to keep it. Within two months, Pastor Kaylor found a new warehouse in Tokyo that he desired to rent for his growing church, but he needed an additional $1,500 dollars a month. When we spoke on the phone, I told him that the watch we had given him was a sign from God that the Lord would provide that exact amount for their new venture of faith.

I have also found it humorous when pastors, in the name of accounting and responsible stewardship, have given me an exact amount of money that came in an offering. Do not be picky with finances or give a guest an exact amount of money figured to the penny, based on your standard for gas reimbursement, for example. Generously round the figure up to a reasonable amount that covers all their expenses and more.

Pastor Klayton Ko of First Assembly of Honolulu and Pastor Rick Seaward of Charismatic Christian Centre in Singapore (an apostle to Pastor Ko and many other churches around the world) both honored us by putting us in beautiful hotel suites and giving us some of the most generous honorariums we have ever received. Pastor Benny Hinn of Orlando, Florida, instructed his youth pastor to give us one of the largest love offerings ever for our ministry when we held a Dragonslayer seminar in his church.

If you want to reap more anointing and more revelation and more harvest of souls, honor the messengers whom God sends to you and bless them. None of us would want to be that innkeeper who had no room in his inn to receive the Savior of the world. We should prepare ourselves to receive the messengers of God in a manner worthy of their calling and worthy of the name of Jesus Christ.

ORAL ROBERTS COMES TO SEATTLE

Recently we had the privilege of hosting Dr. and Mrs. Oral Roberts at our church. Having the Robertses there was like hosting the New Testament apostles in our church. The story of their stay with us illustrates the message I am attempting to convey here.

We made special arrangements to care for the then-81-year-old Dr. Roberts and his wife, Evelyn, during their brief stay in Seattle. Four of us arrived early at the airport to welcome them. Our generation pastor, Jude Fouquier, an Oral Roberts University graduate, and I went early and met the couple at the gate as they deplaned. Jude took Sister Evelyn's arm and gently walked her all the way to the car, while Brother Roberts and I chatted along the way. We ushered them out to a waiting Mercedes, where our elders Don and Marlene Ostrom were prepared to drive the couple to their hotel. With a description of their bag, Jude and I retrieved it while the Robertses relaxed in the car.

Glenda Renes, our very efficient church administrator, had preregistered our guests and had obtained the key to their special suite in one of Seattle's finest hotels along the waterfront of Lake Washington. This enabled the Ostroms to walk them directly to their room without delay. The Robertses then rested a short time until dinner. The meal was finely prepared and served in their suite, around a table, ensuring the privacy and intimacy they desired.

After a wonderful meal and time of fellowship, we prayed together for their ministry the next day, and we briefly discussed the plan for the service. Dr. Roberts blessed each of us and then retired early.

The next morning, we started our day with a dynamic prayer meeting around our church's altars, with several hundred people praying fervently for the special meeting. Additional ushers were readied to serve, for security purposes, at the head of every aisle, on the sides of the auditorium and in the front. They received instructions and prayer to be alert and on watch during this special meeting.

Dr. and Mrs. Roberts were picked up at their hotel by the Ostroms, welcomed at the church by our ushers, and escorted safely through my private office entrance and into my office, where they were hosted until the meeting began. We prayed together and then walked, escorted by strong ushers, through side doors into the main auditorium where the service had already started.

The service was electric with an atmosphere of faith and expectation. The worship was well planned, including a rousing

rendition of "It Is Well with My Soul." The choir sang beautifully and, by the end of worship, the people were ready to receive
the Word of God.

Pastor Jude, who described a very brief but dynamic overview
of Dr. Roberts' life and ministry, made the formal introduction
and introduced a video clip of one of Roberts' tent meetings
from 1955. I then shared with our people what a great privilege
it was to have a man of Dr. Roberts' stature at City Church. The
congregation gave him a standing ovation.

At the end of a dynamic and penetrating message, Dr.
Roberts and I both prayed for the people, and many stood and
received words of healing and deliverance. We finished the service with a love offering for our guests, and the people liberally
gave an offering of nearly $25,000.

As Dr. and Mrs. Roberts were escorted to their car and taken
to the airport by our elders, the couple remarked repeatedly how
they had enjoyed their time with us, what a miracle the Lord had
done in the church and how grateful they were for our generosity. I thought to myself, *This is how we would have treated any of the
great men or women of Church history, had we had the chance.* On this
day, we had the opportunity and took advantage of it, and we
could look forward to receiving a prophet's reward and a harvest
back from the seed of love and hospitality we planted in faith.

KEEPING THE FIRE BURNING

by Sergio Scataglini

Sergio Scataglini recently stepped down as senior pastor of Puerta del Cielo church in La Plata, Argentina, to focus on reaching the nations through his speaking ministry. God has given to Sergio a ministry to impart to others a passion for a life of holiness, including the members of Harvest Rock Church. He has had a profound impact on thousands who have heard him speak. This chapter is adapted from his book The Fire of His Holiness *(Ventura, CA: Renew Books, 1999).*

The LORD is with you when you are with Him.
And if you seek Him, he will let you find Him; but if you
forsake Him, He will forsake you.

2 CHRONICLES 15:2, *NASB*

One evening a pastor friend of mine stopped by our home. "I invite you to go with me to Pastor Raul's house for dinner tonight!" he said, insisting that we join them. A cookout was planned, so we brought some meat and vegetables and some of our own plates and silverware and went to Raul's house. As it turned out, Raul was not expecting so many of us. He did have a fire going, however, so I cooked the meat on the grill, while the ladies prepared the salads and vegetables. Raul's family was able to host us because we had brought a good deal of food and helped to prepare the meal.

This is how we are able to host the Holy Spirit. We offer to Him what He has brought with Him. We set before Him a plate that He has given us and serve on the table the things He has graciously provided for us. Do you want to host the Holy Spirit? Accept what He brings to the table. Let Him do the cooking. Seek after the fire of His holiness.

Many Christians believe that if only they are holy enough, the Spirit of God will *want* to come and stay with them. This is like a child who believes his parents will stay with him because he makes his bed and brushes his teeth. Faithful parents will stay with their young children, whether the kids do these things or not. Out of this secure relationship between parent and child flow effective correction and training and a response of obedience and compliance. By yielding to our heavenly Father's will and making ourselves available to His process of purification in our lives, we invite the Holy Spirit to come and remain with us.

When I first received the baptism of the fire of His holiness, my friend Claudio Freidzon told me, "This fire will never leave you." To this day I believe with all my heart that this is possible, that the presence of the Lord can come and remain for more than a sporadic visitation.

FIRE, BURN BRIGHTLY!

An integral part of being Argentine is grilling and eating good meat. One of the most common social phenomena in Argentina is the *asado*—a meat cookout. For our honeymoon, my wife, Kathy, and I had chosen to spend our first week together in a cabin in Yosemite National Park. One afternoon, we decided to have a cookout for supper.

I began gathering the wood and just the right kind of kindling. I even chose some pine cones to use. Kathy sat nearby, observing me as I gathered a pile of things that I would need for our first cookout as husband and wife. I do not believe that my wife, a native of Indiana, had ever seen food cooked over a fire that was not built out of charcoal and lighter fluid.

You can imagine my intense desire to make that fire work, not only so we could cook our food but also so my wife would be impressed by her industrious husband. After arranging the materials just right, I soon had a nice fire crackling. I find it a personal challenge to build the perfect fire, even today, for our cookouts.

Once the fire is started, however, I tend to say to myself, *Well, that was the hard part; now I can relax.* But sure enough, if I leave for a few minutes, the fire will die down. And that is the way it is with the holy fire of God. If we are not careful with this precious flame, it can become neglected. Following are some principles that will help you keep the fire of His presence burning in your life and in your church.

BELIEVE THE LORD HAS CALLED YOU TO BE 100% PURE

If you do not believe in the calling of purity, that is where the danger will come. Satan will persuade you that 1% or 2% sin is all right, as though it were milk fat. He will say, "After all, you live in the real world in modern times. You are not expected to live a completely holy life." If you allow him, the devil will deceive you.

I pray that the Lord would give you conviction today and that your mind would be renewed. I pray that from this day until the day that Jesus comes, you will declare war against every kind of evil. You will need to become a terrible enemy of sin. You will need to fight it on all counts.

As I was in the presence of the Lord, God spoke to me in terms that even a child could understand. (At that moment, I could not understand anything more complex than that.) He told me, "Nobody gets up in the morning and prepares a cup of coffee or tea and puts just one drop of poison in it, then stirs and drinks it." Then He began to speak to me about the Church. There are people in the Church who allow poison into their hearts and into their minds and it is destroying them.

Sometimes we indulge in apparently insignificant sins. So many people wonder, *Why do I lose the power of God or the strength of the Lord so quickly? Maybe it is because I am a failure, or maybe it is because I am not trained.* I tell you that when sin is allowed to taint even 1% of our lives, it can eventually destroy our whole devotion.

Some of you are afraid of this. You say, "I have heard people preach against immorality, and they ended up falling into immorality themselves." Sadly, in part this is true, and you may think that those who talk too much about holiness will fall into sin. But you must know that many of those who fell were redeemed again and that many who preached against immorality their entire lives did not fall. Remember Moses? Elijah? Elisha? Daniel? Jeremiah? They preached fervently against sin and idolatry and, though they may have stumbled, they remained faithful.

The Word of God is our example; experience is not our rule. How can our experience give us the right answers if we have been on the wrong path with the wrong kind of understanding? That is like giving our car keys to an auto thief and asking him to keep an eye on our vehicle while we go shopping. Wrong experience, like a car thief, cannot be trusted.

Do you believe the Word of God? Are you certain that Jesus truly came to Earth, that His body was not made out of plastic, that He was real? Do you believe He endured temptation and hunger and yet did not say yes to sin on any account? If so, you are following the right path. When tempted by the enemy, Jesus said, "Satan, it is written." With the Word of the Lord, He fought sin and evil (see Luke 4). You can do the same thing. You and I are *called* to do the *same thing!*

Christian means "little Christ," follower of Christ, imitator of Jesus Christ. It has to be very clearly established in our hearts and minds: We are called to absolute purity, just like our model, Christ.

> May the God of peace Himself sanctify you completely; and may your whole spirit, soul, and body be preserved blameless at the coming of our Lord Jesus Christ (1 Thess. 5:23).

This verse is talking about complete and total sanctifying power. Our sanctification must be total, from our heads to our toes. Every cell of our bodies should be sanctified by the Word of God. Every thought and action should be purified by Jesus. Some people say, "Pastor, I wish I could do this, but I am weak and shy and suffer from doubt." But:

> The one who calls you is faithful and he will do it (1 Thess. 5:24, *NIV*).

The demands of God have not been lowered in this century. God demands that each one of us live in absolute purity. You can call it pride; you can call it excess; you can call it extravagance. But the Bible tells us that by the time Jesus comes, the whole Church should be pure, waiting in ready expectation for Him.

To keep humble, some people leave a little sin in their lives because they do not want to be too holy, too pure or too spiritual. Let me ask you a question: Can a human being be too pure before a holy God? Do you think God would say, "Don't come and pray like that; you are too clean. See if you can get some filth on you so you look more human, and then come back"?! God Almighty loves us and desires that we be totally pure.

How do we become holy? The One who calls us is faithful, and He will do it through us. It is in the power of the Holy Spirit that we become holy.

KEEP GIVING AWAY THE FIRE OF GOD

If you receive a baptism of fire and all you do is stay home and do nothing about it, you will lose it very quickly. Why do they call the Dead Sea a dead sea? Because it takes in water from different rivers and streams, but it has no outlets. The water disperses only through evaporation, so the sea (technically it is a very large lake) accumulates salt. There is so much salt that no fish can live there. No tree can grow at its banks.

Some Christians are like the Dead Sea. They go to the best conferences and they receive and receive and the salt accumulates. But instead of being the "salt of the earth" (Matt. 5:13), they are the salt of themselves and they keep piling it up—more books, more tapes, more videos, more knowledge. They increase and grow but do not reach out.

Carlos Annacondia, the Argentine evangelist, says it so well: "If we want to keep the anointing, we have to keep giving it away." Every person in the Body of Christ is a minister. We are all called to be a special people of God, ministers and servants of the Lord God Almighty.

UNDERSTAND THAT HOLINESS IS NOT AN END IN ITSELF

My friend and mentor Ed Silvoso tells us why it does not make sense to pursue holiness as the ultimate end: "If the only thing God wanted from us was to be holy, then we might as well drop dead right now and be with God in heaven. We are going to be more holy there than we are anyplace else!" But the goal is not only to be holy, but to be holy *so that* we are a holy nation, a chosen people. We are a people special to God; we are set apart. For what? To *declare* the praises of Him who called us out of darkness (see 1 Pet. 2:9).

In the theology of holiness, we find two key aspects: separated from the world and separated to serve God. Separation must be accompanied by a dedication to serve.

Victorious Christian living is not only living on the defense, but it is also being armed and ready to advance. We cannot win a basketball game simply by staying close to the hoop to protect it. The best we could hope for using this tactic is a 0-0 tie. We have to run to the other end of the court and sink a few baskets to win the game.

THE BAPTISM OF FIRE IS FOR THE FULFILLMENT OF THE GREAT COMMISSION

Every Christian has heard that the mandate of the Great Commission is to "go into all the world and preach the good

news to all creation" (Mark 16:15, *NIV*). Nothing will help us fulfill the Great Commission faster than receiving a baptism of
fire—the presence of God. This will restore your passion for God
and for lost souls. Those who get rid of their sin and receive the
baptism of the Holy Spirit and fire will be in a place to allow
Him to do His work in their lives.

A revival focused on the Great Commission will be a blessing
as it brings the message of Jesus Christ to the world. The passage
of Scripture that is known as the Greatest Commandment says
(1) love God and (2) love your neighbor as yourself (see Matt.
22:36-40). The more we love people and the more we pray for
them, the more the fire will burn in our own lives.

The fire that I received could have been lost within a few
days. But the Lord opened opportunities and doors for me to
share this fire, and we took advantage of most of them.
Whenever we had the chance, my wife, Kathy, and I walked
through those doors and ministered to whomever we could.

PRACTICE PERSONAL EVANGELISM

How beautiful it is when you are sitting on a bus, train or air-
plane and God interrupts your agenda. You are getting ready to
take a nap and you tell yourself, *I am so tired. I really deserve this
rest*. But then the Holy Spirit tells you that you need to speak to
the person next to you. You may say, *Lord, can I talk to them after
my nap?* But you sense the love of Christ flowing through your
heart. It is not just a command. You are looking for opportunities and if you are a little timid, you may pray, *Lord, have this person ask me what religion I am, or something like that*. Finally, something happens and the Lord provides the opportunity and you
begin to talk.

In our ministry many people have received Christ on airplanes and in taxis. In Argentina, taxis are a way of life and, typically, they are relatively inexpensive. Sometimes I say to myself, *I am not going to witness to this cabby because I need to rest on this short trip to the office.* And then the love of the Lord begins to flow. He loves people more than we ever will. Before I realize it, within two minutes I am in the middle of a big conversation about Jesus Christ.

I remember one young taxi driver who was taking me home. When we arrived at my house, he turned off the engine (rare for a cab driver!) and right there on my street asked me if I would pray with him. He received Jesus Christ while sitting in his taxi!

A few years back, the Lord impressed upon me that I had never witnessed to one particular neighbor. Finally I decided, *I have got to witness to these people.* So I knocked on the door and a lady answered. I said to her, "Do you know what the Lord has done for me? The power of the Lord came upon me and I was shaking under His mighty anointing."

You and I know that unbelievers do not understand these things. Nevertheless, she said, "Please come in. I need to hear this." She said to her daughters, "Turn off the TV. We need to hear this." For about an hour I witnessed to her and she came to Christ right there in her living room.

Even if you work in full-time ministry, do not let that deter you from the joy of bringing souls, one by one, to Jesus Christ. I know some leaders who tell me, "I do not have time to witness one-on-one. I can be more effective speaking at large conferences." The Lord wants to break this type of professionalism and to remind us that we need to be led by the Spirit moment by moment. Keep giving away to others the fire and blessings that you have received.

KEEP YOUR PASSION FOCUSED ON GOD—
DO NOT IDOLIZE METHODS

One time when the Lord had me in His presence, He began to speak to my heart about making idols out of my methods. Then He sent me to speak to some pastors about church growth and how we must be careful not to abuse it. I was fearful to talk to these pastors about it, because I enjoy studying church growth. But the Lord showed me that some of those ministers were idolizing church growth to the point of making it their obsession and passion. (I use "idolize" here to mean "excessive admiration.")

On my knees, I cried out to the Lord and said, "Oh my God, many of us are looking toward Korea and the tremendous amount of church growth they have experienced. How can I go to these leaders and tell them to be careful about making an idol out of church growth?"

Do you know what the Lord spoke to my heart? He said, "My son, what I did in Korea cannot even be compared to what I am going to do on planet Earth in the coming years."

We have to believe in not only what God has done in the past but also what He is about to do in the future. God wants to bring a knowledge of His glory that covers the earth as the waters cover the seas.

DIVINE INTERVENTION OUTWEIGHS
HUMAN METHODS

You may be thinking, *My church has doubled without ever experiencing the wild kinds of things I am reading about in this book.* But can you imagine what would happen to your already-growing church if it were to receive a visitation of the Holy Spirit? Please, my friend, do not sell your spiritual birthright for a cup of lentil soup! Do not trade the fire of God for nice, steady growth. Pursue both, but know that a true baptism of fire generates true growth. Give priority to pursuing the presence of the Holy Spirit.

Normal church growth occurs when we share the gospel with the lost around us. This is wonderful and biblical. It is the law of God, and we should continue doing it. But there is also a miraculous, explosive supernatural growth that happens when the Holy Spirit descends upon a nation. This is not a method but a movement. The people in your neighborhood will begin to say, "Did you see what God is doing with those Christians?"

DO NOT GIVE UP ON YOUR SPIRITUAL DREAMS

How many of us have dreamt for years about a day when the move of God would be so great that we would have to stand back and marvel at His glorious work? It does not matter what kinds of barriers or failures you have experienced in the past. It does not matter if you are timid or afraid. It does not matter that you may have been a failure in the past. You must go to the source and receive this fire and authority.

If you go for the fire, you will need to be like Jacob when he took hold of the feet of the Angel of the Lord and said, "I will not let You go unless You bless me!" (Gen. 32:26). You must tell the Lord, "I am tired of working in my own strength. I want the strength of Your Spirit. I want to walk in the Spirit, be full of the Spirit and fire and have the mind of Jesus Christ. Lord, change my ministry!" He will do it!

GO TO THE EXTREMES FOR HOLINESS

Perhaps you do not struggle with sexual temptation. But those of us that are very human have to be very careful. Oftentimes, by the time I get back to my hotel room after a long, wonderful meeting, I am drained. I am physically exhausted and weak. I know that I am not a good fighter when I am very tired. Many of you can relate. We are human. On this side of heaven, we are vulnerable; our strength is limited.

Because of this human weakness, the Lord has helped me to develop a habit that has been a blessing to me. No matter where I am in the world, the first thing I do when I enter my hotel room is drop my luggage, close the door, kneel down and ask God to take over that room. I pray for forgiveness for any fornication, adultery, immorality or pornography that has been present in that room before my arrival. Then I stand and command the demons that had legal right to stay in that room to get out. That room becomes the house of God while I am there.

I then take one of those big hotel towels or one of the blankets, and I cover the TV. And since I usually carry two Bibles, one in Spanish and one in English, I open one and place it on the TV, which then becomes the podium upon which I prepare my messages. The Bible says, "Flee from sexual immorality" (1 Cor. 6:18, *NIV*). This is one way of fleeing—refusing to watch TV while I am at a conference.

IT IS BETTER TO GO TO HEAVEN WITHOUT CABLE TV THAN TO GO TO HELL WITH A WHOLE ENTERTAINMENT CENTER AROUND YOU.

When I began putting a towel over the television in my hotel room, I felt good about it. I thought, *That is one less battle I will have to fight.* Some of you might be saying, "Why would you do that? What is wrong with TV?" I am not saying there is anything wrong with TV. There *is* something wrong with immorality, and there is a lot of immorality on TV. When I am exhausted, it is very hard for me to control the remote control. I do not trust myself that much. I trust the Lord, and the Lord tells me to flee from youthful passions (see 2 Tim. 2:22). So I stay away from television when I am alone. Fight immorality with everything you have; the Lord will do the rest.

Make sure you clean your house of anything that is evil. The Lord tells us to go to extreme measures so that we do not fall into sin. Some of you may have a rough time controlling the cable stations on your TV. You have the blessing of having access to many fine channels, but when you are alone, you cannot control what you watch. You say to yourself, *I am not going to watch this anymore.* Yet when you are alone, you end up watching it. Then you end up feeling so guilty, so filthy—I am talking about evil programs, not good programs.

I would like to share with you my paraphrase of Matthew 5:29: If cable TV is giving you an occasion to fall, it is better to unplug the TV set and cancel the cable service and go to heaven without cable than to go to hell with a whole entertainment center around you!

DEVELOP NEW HABITS OF GODLINESS

We need to change our habits. Some experts say that it takes 16 days to change a habit. Some of you will have to work for at least

16 days, keeping a straight line until your flesh gets the message. You must commit that in His power, you are going to pursue righteousness, purity and holiness—and you must mean it! Until our minds are renewed, the old wineskins remain. But when we are renewed in our minds, the new wineskins come and the new wine is poured into the new wineskins. Job 31:1 (*NIV*) says: "I made a covenant with my eyes not to look lustfully at a girl." We must do the same.

Preachers, teachers, evangelists, brothers and sisters, today we must sign a covenant with our eyes. We have to tell our eyes, "You are never, ever going to look lustfully at a man or woman." If the person you are looking at is much younger, treat her as if she were your daughter and pray for her as a father. If she is not a Christian, pray for her salvation. If she is a woman your own age, treat her like your sister and with absolute purity. If you do not believe that you can keep such a commitment without help, then find an accountability partner to pray for you and support you.

Again, no one would consider buying a bottle of water with a label that reads: "98% Mountain Spring Water; 2% Sewage Water." You would not decide, *Oh, this is great! It is almost pure. I think I will buy it and drink it*. The Lord wants and demands 100% holiness from us.

FLEE FROM IMMORALITY

When you are running away from something or someone, you do not look very dignified. One time while waiting for a flight, a smiling young woman came walking toward me to talk to me. As she approached, I decided that I was going to witness to her. But something different was happening. As she was walking toward me, the Holy Spirit began to warn me, "I did not send this young lady to you."

The fear of God came upon me. Perhaps "terror" would be a more accurate word. I thought, *Lord, I do not want to become another casualty in Your kingdom.* So, as she came within a few feet, I turned around and literally fled in the opposite direction. She probably thought, *What is wrong with this guy?* I do not really care what she thought. I felt that I was fleeing from something that might have led to a compromising situation (see Gen. 19:17; Isa. 48:20; Jer. 51:6; 1 Cor. 6:18; 1 Tim. 6:11; 2 Tim. 2:22).

Run away from immorality, like Joseph did. Joseph the patriarch was determined that he was not going to commit adultery with Potiphar's seductive wife. When Joseph spurned her advances, she then accused him falsely, and he lost his job (see Gen. 39). Some of you may lose your jobs for walking straight with the Lord. You may lose some worldly riches when you refuse to lie or comply with evil. But do not worry. The Lord will repay you because He is faithful.

Did you know that you can be single and still be pure? The Lord will give you the strength. When the Holy Spirit comes upon you, you will be very strong. You will know, *I am weak, but the Holy Spirit is strong in me.* Marriage does not cure the vice of lust; only the blood of Jesus does. But you need a heart with a disposition toward total purity.

GET CLOSE TO ANOINTED PEOPLE

We have been so careful not to idolize other people that sometimes we do not make ourselves available to receive what they have to give us. If you know a brother or sister who is ablaze with the fire of God, get close to that person. Make friends with the friends of the Bridegroom. The friends of the Bridegroom have lamps that are full of oil and are ready for the moment. Receive from these people and be renewed through them.

It is so powerful when God's children link together in unity and support. If you allow yourself to be vulnerable and to learn from Him and others, the Lord will bless your life and your anointing will increase. You will not lose it. When you think you are losing it, one of your friends will come, guided by the Holy Spirit, and say, "How are you doing? Let's pray together."

If you desire to walk in His purity, take a moment and pray this prayer right now:

God, forgive me for departing from the teaching of holiness. Change my thinking. Help me to believe that Jesus died for my sanctification. Lord, I declare that I can be pure, because Jesus has provided sanctification to me. Lord, I receive the gift of purity, in every area of my life.

The Lord is putting a mark on your heart. With the power of the Holy Spirit, He is sealing the concept that you and I will walk in absolute purity the rest of our lives. Some people say, "What happens if I pray today and then tomorrow I fall into sin again?" You kneel down wherever you are and say, "God, forgive me and purify me." If you have to do it 100 times a day, do it 100 times a day. The Lord will purge you of your sin. He will give you victory and a ministry full of His power.

Some of you may have serious doubts about whether you were destined by God to have this fire. You may think, *I was not born in Argentina* (i.e., a place of ongoing revival), *so maybe I will not receive the fire*. The Lord will always say yes to those who want the Holy Spirit and fire. What I have, I want to give to you. Even as I write these words, I pray that the baptism of fire which I have received would come upon each and every one of you who asks for it and truly desires it.

Together with that fire comes a responsibility to serve God in your city. Are you ready? Are you willing? Please pray this prayer:

Lord, I promise I will use this fire of holiness to minister to the needy, the poor and the sick; to those who don't know You; to my relatives, my friends, even my enemies. Jesus, I promise to use this fire for the glory of Your name and for the extension of Your kingdom. Amen, amen and amen.

We have been taken out of mediocrity and called to be heroes for Christ. Some people desire that the Lord would do something great and that He would do it beginning with them. The Holy Spirit told me that He wants us to die to the pride of originality. Some people try to come up with a strategy that is original to them, and for that reason they will not cooperate with the strategies of others. Some wonder why they do not triumph. Just take hold of Jesus Christ and you will triumph. But you cannot do it with pride. Be holy!

PREACH HOLINESS, AVOID PERFECTIONISM

How can you preach a message of holiness and repentance without becoming judgmental, critical and legalistic? The answer: if you preach with a broken heart. Preach with tears in your eyes. Preach with a heart full of compassion.

Teach that when the Holy Spirit comes upon us, he empowers us to be holy. Holiness comes from Him. It is imparted unto us miraculously. It is not something we can produce with our nature. It is a miracle from God.

In his book *Secrets of the Most Holy Place*, Don Nori shares so beautifully a concept that categorically defeats the notion of perfectionism:

> Your striving is over, your war is over and your struggling is over. You are accepted in the Beloved. Your consciously making an end to all striving demonstrates to Him that you believe. It is at this point, where you purposefully stop working for approval and realize that you are approved, that you truly become a believer. You always thought acceptance and approval were so elusive, but your abandoned, almost reckless (by human standards) refusal to be ruled by the flesh demonstrates that you believe His blood is sufficient.
>
> You now begin to see your service to Him in a wonderful light. Your service is not to gain or attain or win. Your service is because you have already attained and you are co-laboring with Him. It is a result of relationship to Jesus and not the means of gaining a relationship. It is not a means of eternal life, but a joyful entering into His labor because you have eternal life.
>
> You see, you have just discovered a monumental secret. Perfection is not a behavior; perfection is a relationship. Perfection was never intended to be measured by how you behave, but by a relationship—a personal, abiding fellowship with the living Lord, Jesus Christ. When perfection flows from a relationship, there is a liberating desire to please the One you love.[1]

We can host the Holy Spirit through holiness, but we reach that holiness through faith. Our job is not to make ourselves holy; that is the work of the Holy Spirit as we allow Him to work in our lives. Rather, our job is to keep ourselves holy, to remain in the holiness that the Holy Spirit brings to our table. Then through serving Him in holiness we shall retain His presence.

> Now to Him who is able to keep you from stumbling, and to present you faultless before the presence of His glory with exceeding joy, to God our Savior, who alone is wise, be glory and majesty, dominion and power, both now and forever. Amen (Jude 24,25).

Note
1. Don Nori, Sr., *Secrets of the Most Holy Place* (Shippensburg, PA: Destiny Image, 1997), n.p.

KEEPING WATCH

by John Kilpatrick

John Kilpatrick, senior pastor of the Brownsville Assembly of God in Pensacola, Florida, has hosted a great move of the Holy Spirit of God since 1995. More than 3 million people from more than 130 nations have since visited the Brownsville revival, where countless men and women have been saved, healed and filled with the power of the Holy Spirit. John has been a blessing to our congregation, and he has become a good friend. Here, he shares powerful insights into past moves of God as recorded in the Scriptures, and he shows us ways to safeguard ourselves from the schemes of the devil that we may keep the presence of the Holy Spirit among us for the long run.

Even in the midst of revival, God's sheep must have a shepherd. In fact, there is no more important time for a pastor to truly shepherd his flock than in the time of revival. Without proper direction and guidance, the house will not be in order, the Holy Spirit will be grieved, and the revival will not be sustained. Jesus is our chief Shepherd; but He has appointed leaders over His flock to keep them in the ways of life.

When sheep in the field do not hear the voice of their shepherd, if they cannot see him, they will begin to regurgitate their food. They will not swallow what they eat, and they can actually starve themselves to death. A shepherd must be present to nurture his sheep. He also must be able to see, to keep watch over the flock and guard against predators. A sheep grazes on all fours and sees from that level. A shepherd is made to stand tall on two legs, so that he can see much farther afield than his sheep. If he cannot see, he cannot protect the flock.

As one who must give account to God for the assembly He has entrusted to me, I take my role as shepherd very seriously, especially with all that has happened and is happening at our church in Pensacola.

THE DEVIL IS WAITING

As I was studying the Word, the Lord showed me eight different times in Scripture when powerful moves of God occurred—and what happened to block, terminate or undermine these visitations of the Holy Spirit. If there is one thing you can count on when revival comes, it is the inevitability of the enemy's attack when God is birthing something in the Spirit.

Let us look at Revelation 12:1-4 (*KJV*):

And there appeared a great wonder in heaven; a woman clothed with the sun, and the moon under her feet, and upon her head a crown of twelve stars: and she being with child cried, travailing in birth, and pained to be delivered. And there appeared another wonder in heaven; and behold a great red dragon, having seven heads and ten horns, and seven crowns upon his heads. And his tail drew the third part of the stars of heaven, and did cast them to the earth: and the dragon stood before the woman which was ready to be delivered, for to devour her child as soon as it was born.

There are many interpretations of this portion of Scripture, but almost all agree that the dragon represents Satan. The devil started off in the Bible as a serpent, and he ends as a dragon. He has grown in power, and he is waiting to devour anything that God is birthing on the earth. Just as the child was getting ready to be born, as one wonder was happening in heaven, another wonder was happening at the same time: The devil was attempting to manifest his power. Whenever God gets ready to move, you can be sure the devil will do the same.

We need to understand that the devil has now had 6,000 years of experience in dealing with humanity. We must not take him for granted or forget his purposes to destroy. The apostle John saw the last days and how the enemy would increase in power, and he warned us of perilous times.

The people of God need to be alert and wise, personally and corporately. We need to understand that the devil is on the prowl, going about as a roaring lion, seeking whom he may devour (see 1 Pet. 5:8). Our enemy is powerful, and we need to put on the whole armor of God (see Eph. 6:11). We must keep our vision sharp and our ears trained to hear the Lord's direction. When a visitation of the Spirit is taking place, we should know that the devil is on the sidelines, drawing up plays that target the vulnerabilities of our preachers, evangelists, staff, volunteers, worship teams, prayer warriors and intercessors. We must be aware of how the enemy tends to attack so that we can stand, safeguarding our hearts, our homes and our churches for the habitation of the Spirit of God.

Let us look now at some mighty moves of God recorded in

Scripture and nine ways the enemy came in before, during or after these moves to rob and destroy the people of God.

1. A SPIRIT OF DECEPTION

> And the LORD said unto Moses, Go, get thee down; for thy people, which thou broughtest out of the land of Egypt, have corrupted themselves: They have turned aside quickly out of the way which I commanded them: they have made them a molten calf, and have worshipped it, and have sacrificed thereunto, and said, These be thy gods, O Israel, which have brought thee up out of the land of Egypt (Exod. 32:7,8, *KJV*).

The children of Israel had been in bondage in Egypt for 300 years when God raised up a man to deliver them. God sent Moses among the Israelites with a powerful rod of authority in his hand, and he was used mightily by God. When Moses cast his rod to the ground, wondrous things happened. Out of Pharaoh's own court, God established a man to move among His people to deliver them, and there was a revival.

Signs and wonders followed, as God sent 10 judgments to afflict Egypt, forcing Pharaoh to relinquish his hold over the children of Israel. They came out of Egypt under the hand of God, and even the sea parted before them. A pillar of fire led the people into the wilderness, where they set up camp to wait while Moses went up the mountain to speak with God. There Moses remained for 40 days.

Meanwhile, in the valley below, even after witnessing the miracles of God, the people quickly turned aside and demanded to have their own way. They fell into deception.

One of the first things that happens during any revival is that the enemy deploys a spirit of deception. Deception is possible. Deception is strong. We are fallen creatures, and we are vulnerable. We may want to think otherwise, but that is the truth. The devil has the ability to deceive you if you are not careful. The Bible says that in the last days even the elect, the Body of Christ, will be deceived, if possible (see Mark 13:22).

You need to know that it is possible for you as a child of God to be deceived, that it is possible for a church to be deceived and that it is certainly possible for a pastor to be deceived. Aaron was. He was the high priest. In the absence of their leader, the people of God began to ask for their own gods. They pressured Aaron. After all, other nations had *their* gods. With Moses on the mountain, the people began to feel abandoned in the wilderness, and a spirit of deception came upon them. This deception was so strong that they convinced the high priest of God to make for them a golden calf—an idol!

God interrupted Himself in the middle of giving the Ten Commandments, and He ordered Moses to return to the people immediately, for they had corrupted themselves and quickly turned aside from what the Lord had commanded them to do.

I am so thankful that God has been visiting us in Pensacola since that Father's Day in 1995. But I am ever aware that if we do not stay close to God and His Word and walk in it with Christ, it won't take long for a spirit of deception to come in and for the devil to deceive us. We are not invulnerable to turning aside quickly, even though the Lord has delivered us with mighty miracles. Though we have seen His manifest presence, though we shake and sense His presence among us, if we are not careful, we will be just like Israel and go seeking after more goodies.

If we lose our focus or begin to stray outside the perimeters of God, we can be all too easily swayed by evil doctrines and evil men. Something that looks good and sounds good and feels good is not always of God. If we remain humble, alert, obedient and wise, I believe we will not be deceived.

Test the spirits to see if they are of God. Look at your heart's motives, and go after that which is of God and not that which is demanded by men.

2. REBELLION

And the children of Israel also wept again, and said, Who shall give us flesh to eat? We remember the fish, which we did eat in Egypt freely. . . . But now our soul is dried away: there is nothing at all, beside this manna, before our eyes (Num. 11:4-6, *KJV*).

As wicked as deception and in many ways more so, rebellion can creep in where God is moving. Look at Israel's attitude toward God's miraculous provision. The Lord gave His people water to drink and manna for bread, even as they wandered in the wilderness. But soon the children of Israel began to complain. They were tired of bread; they wanted meat.

How many of us have ever turned up our nose at a salvation message, telling God, "I don't want another salvation message. I want meat!" How many of us have ever neglected the miracle of the provision of the Word of God, demanding we have something else, something more? I am not saying that meat is not good. We are indeed to grow in God and to desire meat (see Heb. 5:12-14). But we had better put to use the meat God gives us lest, like the leftover manna, the worms destroy it, and we become corrupt (see Exod. 16:19,20).

Ungrateful hearts can lead to overt disobedience. God was

angered by the Israelites' rebellious attitude, but He nevertheless answered their cry and sent quail for His people to eat. But soon their rebellious attitude worsened into open contempt. Numbers 16 tells the story.

Moses and Aaron were God's appointed leaders for the journey to the Promised Land. But certain men among the Israelites became insolent and spoke out against God's anointed. Dathan and Abiram were among those who incited the people to rebellion; but when Moses summoned them to hear their complaints, they refused. Instead, they belittled Moses and accused him of setting himself up to be a prince over Israel, and of taking too much responsibility: "Isn't it enough that you have brought us up out of a land flowing with milk and honey to kill us in the desert? And now you also want to lord it over us?" (Num. 16:13, NIV). They even accused him of failing to lead the people into the things of God: "Moreover you haven't brought us into a land flowing with milk and honey or given us an inheritance of fields and vineyards" (v. 14). The rebellion of Dathan and Abiram angered God, and the consequences were severe.

We are not so different from the tribes of Israel. Many people today have a problem with a pastor setting limits in their church. For example, I carefully screen our altar workers who pray over people, and there are some people I will not allow to hold that position. When you pray for someone and lay hands on them, you impart something of who you are, something that you possess. If you are not anointed by God or are moving in the flesh, you can do more harm than good. So if someone wants to be a part of our ministry team, he or she must submit to leadership. If that person will not obey our instructions and honor how we pray for people, he or she will not be allowed to participate on the ministry team. Persons with an independent spirit who insist on doing things their own way do not have a place with us.

When rebellion arose in Israel's camp, God dealt with it so that rebellion would not pollute the whole nation. The earth yawned and swallowed up the arrogant, willful men, along with all their possessions and families (see Num. 16:31-33). Rebellion is a serious issue. You cannot have rebellion in your heart in the midst of revival and not affect others. You must humble yourself under the mighty hand of God and under the leadership that has been set over you. Trust that God is dealing with the leadership in your church, and honor God by honoring them.

Do not be like Dathan and Abiram and try to take matters into your own hands. God has given us ways to approach our leadership if we have a disagreement, and that is the course of action that God will honor. The Holy Spirit will take wings and fly from where there is rebellion. We must check our hearts and motives and deal with our wrong attitudes if we want a visitation of God to continue.

3. EVIL SPEAKING

Likewise also these dreamers defile the flesh, reject authority, and speak evil of dignitaries (Jude 8).

Evil speaking seems to go hand in hand with the rejection of authority. Whether it is the evil speaking of Dathan and Abiram or any other as mentioned in Scripture, evil speaking usually ends in disaster. Yet whenever revival comes, people begin to spread rumors and speak evil against those God is using to shepherd and usher in the revival. Incredibly, people who never paid any attention to your church suddenly have opinions about how you run your ministry, what you do, where you go and how you live.

I am amazed at the things I hear about our church these days! Some say that our evangelist Steve Hill is living the life of a millionaire, while others claim that my house is on the market and that I'm getting ready to build a big, new house. People point to the beautiful thing that is happening in Pensacola and they say, "They're making money hand over fist!" This is evil because there is no truth to it. People who spread such rumors are casting aspersions on the people of God and polluting the beauty of what God is doing in revival. They are willing to focus on anything other than God's presence and the wonderful salvation, healing and miracles that the Lord is giving to His people.

The Bible tells us not to receive an evil report about leadership from just one person but to require at least two or three witnesses (see 1 Tim. 5:19). There is a protocol to follow if someone has a question or a problem about leaders God is using in a movement (see Matt. 18:15-17). We must be careful not to give heed to idle gossip, destructive lies and rumors spread with the enemy's wrath and fleshly jealousy. We must prove to be wise peacemakers with those who are misinformed, and avoid those who are foolish.

We must guard what has been entrusted to us by the Holy Spirit and not take part in evil speaking and slander. The Holy Spirit will depart when people destroy the work of God with their tongues. Trust God and have confidence that He will deal with His leaders and judge them if they are out of order. They are His charge and His responsibility.

4. SEXUAL SIN

And it came to pass in an eveningtide, that David arose from off his bed, and walked upon the roof of the king's house: and from the roof he saw a woman washing herself; and the woman was very beautiful to look upon. And David sent and inquired after the woman. And one said, Is not this Bathsheba, the daughter of Eliam, the wife of Uriah the Hittite? And David sent messengers, and took her; and she came in unto him, and he lay with her (2 Sam. 11:2-4, *KJV*).

A great kingdom had been established in the time of King David. A mighty revival had taken place, and David had come to the throne. Saul was dead; David's nemesis was gone. It was a time of peace. In fact, it was so peaceful that David made an unwise decision not go to war with his armies. He chose to let God watch over the troops because things were going so well. He decided to stay home and send out his armor bearer in his place.

WHAT ARE YOU DOING WITH YOUR TIME? INVEST WISELY. BE ABOUT THE WORK OF THE LORD.

He let down his guard and relaxed "at the time when kings go out to battle" (2 Sam. 11:1).

In the midst of revival, when you think everything is fine, you need to be on the alert! Just because souls are being saved, the church is growing and tithes and offerings are on the rise, don't think for a second that the devil is going to leave you alone.

Allow me to be straightforward with you. In the midst of revival, be careful. Keep your passions harnessed. Adultery is one of Satan's most powerful ploys. If he can, he will walk right up to you, put a hook in your jaw and lead you astray down the primrose path of sexual promiscuity. The Bible tells us that David stayed home and did not go to war. What are you doing in the midst of revival? Watching television? Goofing off? You are vulnerable! Invest your time wisely; be about the work of the Lord.

Don't be casual about God's presence being poured out on your church. Stay involved. Many people relax after awhile and quit coming to the meetings—they stop pursuing the presence of God. During a time of revival, you are more vulnerable to temptation than ever, and you need to know that.

Be circumspect and give the devil no opportunity. Be careful what you watch. Be careful whom you are with. Be careful to do what the Lord wants you to be doing and not what your flesh would choose. Be aware that idle time is one of the enemy's favorite tools and sexual immorality one of his most effective diversions from the things of God.

Guard your eyes and your heart.

5. A JEZEBEL SPIRIT

And Ahab told Jezebel all that Elijah had done, and withal how he had slain all the prophets with the sword. Then Jezebel sent a messenger unto Elijah, saying, So let the gods do to me, and more also, if I make not thy life as the life of one of them by to morrow about this time. And when he saw that, he arose, and went for his life (1 Kings 19:1-3, *KJV*).

A Jezebel spirit is a serious matter and not something to be played with. It can zero in on a leader and actually render him or her useless in the ministry.

Revival was sweeping the land. With a dramatic demonstration of the power of the living God, the prophet Elijah had humiliated and embarrassed the 450 prophets of Baal. Seeing this, the people cried out, "The LORD, He is God! The LORD, He is God!" (1 Kings 18:39). Elijah then executed the false prophets. But there was a woman nearby who was full of the devil and who lurked in the midst of that great revival.

Queen Jezebel promised that she would have the head of God's prophet. The runners came to Elijah and told him of her murderous intent, her words carrying the strong spirit of Jezebel upon them. So, during the greatest revival he had ever seen, Elijah ran away and hid in the wilderness, depressed and discouraged. He did not even want to live (see 1 Kings 19:4).

Be alert in the midst of revival. One of the greatest weapons the devil will use against you in these last days is a severe attack of the blues. A Jezebel spirit is almost like a curse, like a witch's spell. A black cloud comes over you and tries to render you useless and ineffective. The devil knew exactly how to get to Elijah, and he dealt with him severely during a time of revival. God sent an angel to Elijah, cooked the prophet a meal and gave him 40 days of rest; but Elijah still could not shake his discouragement. God busted rocks. God sent a fire. God sent an earthquake. God spoke to him in the still small voice. But Elijah did not change his mind.

I believe this may have been the end of his effective ministry. The Lord instructed Elijah to leave the wilderness, and He sent the prophet to go and anoint Elisha as his successor. God still loved Elijah, and He rewarded him by taking the prophet to heaven in a chariot of fire; but Elijah's ministry was rendered ineffective and useless by the Jezebel spirit.

If you don't think a Jezebel spirit is still around today, take a look at Revelation 2:20, wherein Christ rebukes the church at Thyatira for tolerating "that woman Jezebel." Jezebel had been killed, and the dogs licked up her blood. Yet we find her in the book of Revelation because this is a spirit. According to the Bible, she tries to "teach and seduce My servants to commit sexual immorality and eat things sacrificed to idols" (Rev. 2:20).

Worship leaders beware. Pastors beware. Sometimes, when I've been under attack, I could hardly stand on the platform—my heart was in my belly. There was nothing wrong in the natural realm. No one had done or said anything to offend or discourage me; but I was under severe attack. However, a double dose of prayer and some "carpet time" caused the dark cloud to be lifted right off me.

You may think that you do not need prayer or that you can fight this thing on your own. I must tell you, the Jezebel spirit is strong, and if you go it alone, the devil is going to pick you off like a sniper. We need each other in time of revival. We need to lay hands on one another. Wake up and say, "God, this is not physical, this is not chemical, this is not a monthly problem. This is an attack of the devil!" Quit blaming everything from the weather to last night's pizza, and recognize the devil's attack for what it is. Then get hands laid on you and get help!

6. THE DISCOURAGEMENT OF HARASSMENT

> But it so happened, when Sanballat heard that we were rebuilding the wall, that he was furious and very indignant, and mocked the Jews. And he spoke before his brethren and the army of Samaria, and said, "What are these feeble Jews doing?" (Neh. 4:1,2).

In 446 B.C., the people of Israel were scattered, and the city of Jerusalem lay in ruins. Nehemiah petitioned the king of Persia to allow him to return to the city of his fathers to rebuild the gates and walls of Jerusalem. The king granted him safe conduct and materials for the task. Answering to a mandate of the Holy Spirit on his life, Nehemiah led a remnant of the Jewish people in an all-out effort to rebuild. He rallied the troops and got his people under the blood, and they built the walls. Nehemiah was being used by God to fulfill a mighty prophecy.

Meanwhile, Sanballat the Horonite and Tobiah the Ammonite were being used by the devil to harass, harangue and intimidate Nehemiah and his people. The whole time Nehemiah and his people worked on the walls, these two men worked devilishly to tear down their spirits, tormenting Nehemiah and the children of Israel. They sent letters. They mocked. They cursed the workers and their handiwork. There were times when their words were so demonic and so oppressive that the workers' heads and hands hung low. Nehemiah constantly had to motivate his men, talking tough at times to keep them going.

Anytime you are in revival, a lot of motivation, a lot of prayer and a lot of pep talks will be needed to keep the people going. Even when you have a mandate from God, and the grace of God is upon you, regular and powerful encouragement will still be required to ward off the harassment of the enemy.

Leaders, be sure you surround yourselves with the right people. An unwise high priest gave a chamber in the Temple to Tobiah, a tormentor and destroyer of the things of God, after he stood outside the walls and spoke against what the Lord was doing (Neh. 13:7)! You will find that, during revival, evil men will be maneuvered by the enemy into a position to infiltrate that revival. If they are able to work their way into the house of God during the revival, they can manipulate the move of God, bring confusion and cause the work to cease.

I thank God that He has sent strong men to work with me at Brownsville. The Lord has given me honest men of integrity to surround the work of God here. I would trust any man on my board of directors to pray for me if I were on my deathbed. Every deacon I have, I trust. They are proven; they are roadworthy; they have been through the storms. They are men of God. I believe that one reason God chose this place to pour out His Holy Spirit is that evil men are not a in a position to disrupt His work.

He has given us a team who can stand arm in arm and face the devil every night. We rejoice together in the Holy Spirit that God has sent generals to lead. But we cannot put on spiritual blinders and allow anything and everything to come in the door. We must try the spirits to see if they are of God. If they are not of God, pastor, stand in your authority and do not allow the wrong people to remain on staff. A Sanballat is so smooth in his words, and Tobiah was so deceptive that he worked his way into close relationship with one of the priests. The priest not only invited the enemy in to see what was going on but also prepared him a chamber right in the house of the Lord.

Shepherds, keep watch.

7. MAN WORSHIP

The three companies blew the trumpets and smashed the jars. Grasping the torches in their left hands and holding in their right hands the trumpets they were to blow, they shouted, "A sword for the LORD and for Gideon!" (Judg. 7:20, *NIV*).

A grievous roadblock to sustaining any move of the Holy Spirit is the worship of any man. Let's look at the story of Gideon, who led the men of Israel to a great and highly improbable victory.

According to the direction of the Lord, Gideon gathered a mere 300 men to go up against an army "as numerous as locusts" whose camels were "as the sand by the seashore in multitude" (Judg. 7:12). And Gideon's strategy for overcoming these staggering odds? Each man of his army was given a trumpet and a clay pitcher with a torch inside. By night, they surrounded the enemy and, at Gideon's signal, they all blew their trumpets and broke their pitchers, allowing the light to shine forth. They shouted and blew their trumpets, and the enemy cried out in confusion, killing one another, while the others fled.

After the greatest victory that Israel had known in Gideon's time, things began to calm down. This is a dangerous time during any move of God.

Let's look at how the people responded:

> Then the men of Israel said unto Gideon, Rule thou over us, both thou, and thy son, and thy son's son also: for thou hast delivered us from the hand of Midian. And Gideon said unto them, I will not rule over you, neither shall my son rule over you: the LORD shall rule over you (Judg. 8:22,23, *KJV*).

Gideon refused to rule; and yet a few verses later, we see that Gideon made a golden ephod and put it in his city. All Israel went whoring after it, worshiping the ephod of Gideon, and it "became a snare unto Gideon, and to his house" (v. 27).

We are not here to make anyone a king except Jesus Christ. It must never be different. People began to say, "Look what Gideon did. Let's exalt him!" Let me tell you something, I haven't got sense enough to run a church. I don't have sense enough to get saved. But the Holy Spirit brought me in, convicted me and got me saved. I didn't find the Lord; He found me.

Even though I can read and I went to Bible school, without the Holy Spirit I know I don't have what it takes to run a church. Any abilities God chooses to use through any of us in Pensacola are His gifts, and they need to be acknowledged as such. The glory goes to no man.

The truth is, I can't heal anybody of any disease. If anyone receives a prophecy from my lips, it did not come from me; it came from the Holy Spirit. If people get saved in our church, I didn't save them. Steve Hill didn't save them. It was the Lord Jesus who saved them.

The Holy Spirit will not be pleased if, when He is moving, people begin to look to any person for the answers, whether it is an evangelist, a pastor, a prophet, an author, a teacher or a prayer leader. Nevertheless, it seems that during any crucial move of God, people begin to start figuring out ways to make somebody king.

I want the Holy Spirit to get the glory so that revival will continue!

8. MONEY PROBLEMS AND COVETOUSNESS

[Naaman's] flesh was restored like the flesh of a little child, and he was clean. And he returned to the man of God . . . and he said, "Indeed, now I know that there is no God in all the earth, except in Israel; now therefore, please take a gift from your servant" (2 Kings 5:14,15).

Naaman, commander of the army of the king of Syria, was a mighty man of valor, but he was also a leper. Having heard stories of a healing prophet in Israel, the king sent gold and silver with his commander and instructed him to find this prophet.

The prophet Elisha did indeed heal Naaman of leprosy; but he refused to take any silver or gold for doing so. Elisha wasn't in this for money. He told Naaman to go on his way and receive his healing (see 2 Kings 5:1-16).

But Gehazi, Elisha's servant, was overcome with a spirit of covetousness—he vowed he would get money from this man. Gehazi caught up with Naaman and concocted a story to receive some silver and clothing in exchange for the man's healing. Gehazi then returned to Elisha. When Elisha asked where he had gone, Gehazi replied, "Nowhere." But Elisha knew what had happened, and he rebuked his servant, "Is this the time to take money and goods?" He then cursed Gehazi, saying that the leprosy of Naaman would now cling to Gehazi and his descendants forever (see 2 Kings 5:20-27).

This was the same man who had stood by Elisha and witnessed many mighty acts of God. This is the same servant who was privileged to see the multitude of angels and fiery chariots all around after Elisha prayed that his eyes would be opened to see them. The sad truth is that even in the midst of a revival where people are seeing the power of God and genuine miracles, they may yet respond with a manifestation of a spirit of covetousness.

This happened even in Jesus' own company. One of His disciples was a devil who always had his hand in the money bag. Judas had a fit when Martha's sister, Mary, used a very expensive perfume to wash Jesus' feet. Indignant at her wastefulness, Judas protested, "Why wasn't this perfume sold and the money given to the poor? It was worth a year's wages" (John 12:5, *NIV*). The Bible tells us that Judas's concern was in fact for the ministry's money, to which he would help himself now and then (see v. 6). He had a covetous spirit. He spent his days in the presence of the greatness of Jesus, seeing all that He did, and yet Judas's focus was still on money.

During the early days of the Church, all the believers were one in heart and mind. No one claimed any of his possessions as his own. They shared everything they had, and there were no needy persons among them:

> For all who were possessors of lands or houses sold them, and brought the proceeds of the things that were sold, and laid them at the apostles' feet; and they distributed to each as anyone had need (Acts 4:34,35).

But when Ananias and Sapphira stepped up to give the proceeds from the sale of some property, they conspired among themselves to keep part of the money for themselves. They lied to the Holy Spirit.

Right in the midst of revival, as thousands of people were being saved and the sick were being miraculously healed, during this mighty outpouring of the power of God, Ananias and Sapphira dared to lie to the Holy Spirit. Peter confronted them, and they both fell dead. A harsh penalty? I believe that if God had not dealt with that covetous spirit with finality then and there, the Early Church might never have developed and matured. A little leaven will leaven the whole lump (see Gal. 5:9).

Be alert: During a great outpouring, the devil will try to distract you with money. He will attempt to get you busy making more money to divert your attention from the things of God. Or he will try to get you to focus on other people's money and what they should be doing with it. He loves to make us question people's motives—especially those of your pastor! If you have covetousness in your heart, beware: It will come out. The devil will help you to project on other people the darkness that may be in your own heart. Let the Lord search you and bring any unresolved money issues to your attention.

9. PASSIVITY

Now it came to pass in the seventh month, that
Ishmael . . . [and the] ten men with him, came unto
Gedaliah the son of Ahikam to Mizpah; and there they
did eat bread together in Mizpah. Then arose Ishmael
the son of Nethaniah, and the ten men that were with
him, and smote Gedaliah . . . with the sword, and slew
him (Jer. 41:1,2, *KJV*).

Passivity is perhaps more insidious than any of the other things we
must guard against during a move of God. When you are lustful,
you can feel the desire. When you are covetous, you are driven to
get more. Depression is often accompanied by physical symptoms.
But this ploy of the enemy you rarely feel or readily recognize.

We find in Jeremiah 40 that when Babylon took the tribes of
Israel into captivity, the king of Babylon left a remnant in Judah
and appointed Gedaliah as governor over them. Those Jews who
remained came to Gedaliah in Mizpah from all the countries
where they had been scattered. Gedaliah was a godly man who
reassured the people and encouraged them to serve the
Babylonians, so that all should be well with the Jews in the land.
And indeed they harvested an abundance of wine and fruit that
year. Things were definitely looking up.

But Gedaliah became complacent. Despite the warnings of a
trusted advisor, he ended up trusting the wrong man, and it cost
him his life (see Jer. 40:14—41:2). When things are going well and
you think you have it all under control, don't be smug. Don't be
passive. Be open to counsel. Be alert and be aware.

Pride will try to slip in. Pride is a horrendous block to the
things of God, and pride makes you blind. If someone approach-
es you with godly counsel, take heed. If you do not listen to godly

counsel, you will be destroyed. Gedaliah, though a godly man, did not take heed. He was resting comfortably in what God was doing in his life, and he felt impenetrable and above being counseled. He did not respond to a word from the Lord, and he was killed by his enemies as a result.

The wonder and awe of revival is no time to rest on your laurels and let your guard down. Instead, it is a time to be all the more alert and guard the things God has entrusted to you. "Be sober, be vigilant; because your adversary the devil walks about like a roaring lion, seeking whom he may devour. Resist him, steadfast in the faith" (1 Pet. 5:8,9). God has given us great counsel in His Word.

May we heed the warnings God has given us in Scripture so that many more will be saved, healed and delivered, that the Holy Spirit will remain among us, and that revival will spread throughout the land.

Hosting the Holy Spirit Through

WALKING IN THE ANOINTING

by Kingsley Fletcher

Kingsley Fletcher recently prophesied to me, saying that I would have an impact in Washington, DC, and that I would be meeting with senators and congressmen. Within a month I was active in The Call DC and was having lunch with several senators! Kingsley is more than a prophet. He is an internationally acclaimed lecturer, television personality and author, not to mention a crowned king from the African nation of Ghana. His ministry has touched more than 70 nations, spanning five continents. Kingsley also serves as senior pastor of Life Community Church in Research Triangle Park, North Carolina, where he lives with his wife, Martha, and their daughters, Anna-Kissel and Damaris Joy. Kingsley is the author of Prayer and Fasting *and* The Power of Covenant.

Talk is cheap and ideas are many, but it is the anointing of God that truly makes the difference in someone's life and ministry. We desperately need His anointing for each and every work, for each and every responsibility, for each and every ministry. When we undertake something that is not backed by the anointing of the Lord, it will usually amount to nothing.

Wanting the anointing and responsibly walking in the anointing will cause the Holy Spirit to abide in our lives and in our churches. Walking in the anointing is not meant to be an occasional experience for the Christian but a way of life.

Even if you use eloquent words of man's wisdom or do church in grand style, if you do not have the anointing of the Lord, these things will not bring any heavenly reward because God only rewards that which He inspires. Whatever is not inspired by the Spirit of the Lord is merely a work of the flesh. Works of the flesh will never be approved of the Lord. We must learn instead to walk in the anointing and to make it the true mark of all we do. We need to make it our aim to perform our ministries and life tasks in the anointing.

The anointing is more than just a feeling of the presence of God. It is the manifest presence of the Holy Spirit *leading* us with all-encompassing wisdom and direction. Jesus gives us our example in Luke 4. Luke's account tells us that Jesus was *full* of the Holy Spirit when He returned from the Jordan. It says He was *led* by the Spirit of the Lord.

I want to emphasize that you can filled by the Holy Spirit and not be led by the Holy Spirit. It is important that we understand that we are filled by the Holy Spirit for a purpose: to do something for God! Too many people are of little value to God because they do nothing with the Spirit inside them. They have received the anointing of God, but they are not led by the Spirit of God. Sadly, they allow themselves to be led by the flesh.

Paul wrote to the Galatian church, "O foolish Galatians, who has bewitched you? You began in the Spirit, but now you have ended up working in the flesh" (see Gal. 3:1,3). You can begin a good work or a good ministry in the Spirit, yet end up in the flesh. We must go instead where the Spirit leads us.

THE SPIRIT LEADS YOU INTO TESTING

Notice the first place that Jesus was led after He was filled with the Spirit. The Bible records that Jesus was led by the Spirit into the wilderness to be tempted by the devil (see Matt. 4:1). You may not like this kind of leading, but you might as well face the fact that when you are full of the Spirit and you allow Him to lead you, the first place He will usually lead you is into trouble! This is how the Lord trains us to use His anointing to overcome difficulties.

Most of us want to be filled with the Holy Spirit, hoping that God will then remove the temptations and troubles from our lives. Why do you think the Holy Spirit is given to us? His anointing is there in part to help you deal with the troubles in your life, to overcome these difficulties with the power to live victoriously!

Now Jesus fasted in the wilderness for 40 days and 40 nights, and the enemy knew that He was hungry. Most of us know what it is like to be extremely hungry. When we are very hungry, we will eat almost anything. We may even eat the wrong things, and if we are not careful, we may eat something that has eternal consequences. Remember the story of the brothers Jacob and Esau? One brother sold his entire birthright to the other for a single meal. We must be careful not to surrender our spiritual rights in order to satiate our physical appetites. We need the anointing to resist this kind of temptation.

Look how Jesus followed the Spirit in obedience. Satan knew that if he could get Jesus to wrongly use His anointing to meet His own needs, to serve His own flesh, he could then take Jesus captive. Jesus did not give in. Even in a moment of extreme hunger and physical weakness, He walked in the anointing. He refused the lies and manipulation of the devil, and He emerged from this testing victorious and stronger than before.

We must note, however, that when these tests ended, the devil left Jesus until "an opportune time" (Luke 4:13). The *King James Version* says the devil "departed from him for a season." This is important to understand when talking about walking in the anointing. Just because a person has the anointing, temptation does not cease! When the enemy attacks and is made to flee, he is already looking for another opportunity to return. That is his game. Winning a single battle does not mean an end to all temptation.

Too many Christians fail and fall because they do not understand this. The enemy knows your weaknesses and your victories, and he is ever looking for ways to make you fail. If he leaves a place, he will go wandering to find a way back.

Be careful when you hear people say that they have forever been delivered from something. Some will say, "I used to be an alcoholic, but when I got filled with the Holy Ghost, I was forever set free from drinking." That is not quite true. That person will have to battle against that weakness through the anointing the rest of his life. The enemy will come back to test him. This doesn't mean he won't win the battle, but it does mean there will always be another test.

Many people regularly experience mental battles in the areas of their weaknesses. They may not yield to the attacks, but Satan will return to them again and again. Whatever the addiction, whatever the sin, he *will* tempt you. His alluring voice will come to an alcoholic at an opportune moment—a time of extreme stress, for example—and say, "Why don't you find a little comfort here? One little drink won't hurt you."

If your problem was lying or cheating and you are now filled with the Holy Ghost, be aware that when you find yourself in financial difficulties or strenuous situations, the enemy will be right there looking to pick up where he left off. He will come back to the very place where once you were weak.

The only time the enemy will leave you permanently is when he is finally chained and cast forever into the bottomless pit. Otherwise, he will still come knocking at your door. You may not be able to stop him from knocking, but you can stop him from coming in!

Satan is almost as persistent about knocking on your door as the Lord is (see Rev. 3:20). The enemy will knock on the door of your heart, the door of your emotions, of your attitudes, of your behavior, of your doubt and even the door of your faith. The enemy merely wants you to open a door. One of the most dangerous things we can do is open the door for the enemy—even a crack. He knows how to break the chain when you peek out. If you give him an inch, he'll take ten.

Please understand that just being Spirit-filled doesn't mean the enemy won't try and use you for his purposes. If you allow him, he will come into your home. He likes competition and a challenge. He especially likes defeating those who have the anointing.

Remember, he will come to call every time he can! Walk circumspectly and turn him away through the anointing.

AFTER TESTING, FILLED WITH POWER

One of the most profound statements in the Bible appears in Luke 4:14: "Then Jesus returned in the power of the Spirit to Galilee." News of Him then spread throughout the countryside. Jesus began teaching in the synagogues, and He was praised by all who heard Him. A new recognition, authority and power emanated from this man.

Jesus *did* something with the anointing. After His testing in the desert, Jesus taught, and He followed the leading of the

Spirit. The Bible records that He went into Nazareth where He had been brought up. He went to synagogue, "as His custom was" (Luke 4:16). This is significant. Jesus Himself went to church. He joined the people of God in corporate prayer and worship. Many people misinterpret 1 John 2:27, which says, in essence, "You have an anointing from the Holy One, and you know all things." This does not mean that if the anointing abides in you, you have no need of anyone else to teach you. Oddly, some people think that being Spirit-filled is a license to stay home because you already know it all! Not only is this a wrong-headed and dangerous attitude, but if you are truly led by the Spirit of God, you will *want* to be with God's people in the house of the Lord. You will want to associate with His Body, to give and take. You will want to *do* something with the anointing.

There is a level of growth and maturity that can only come from corporate interaction. We need to value what others have gone through and what they have learned. We too must share what the Spirit is teaching us, so that our discernment and wisdom can grow.

Jesus was in the Temple, declaring that what the Spirit was showing Him. With the revelation and leading of the anointing of God, He could openly declare, "The Spirit of the LORD is upon Me, because He has anointed Me to preach the gospel to the poor; He has sent Me to heal the brokenhearted, to proclaim liberty to the captives and recovery of sight to the blind, to set at liberty those who are oppressed; to proclaim the acceptable year of the LORD" (Luke 4:18,19).

Jesus shared this revelation from the Spirit of God while He was in church and reading the Scriptures. The anointing will lead you *toward* the people of God and His Church, not away from them.

Take a moment to measure the anointing on your life. How often do you go to the house of the Lord? How often do you yield yourself to those who are spiritual for their discernment? Are you following what the Scriptures say?

King David sang that he was glad to go into the house of the Lord (see Ps. 122:1). When you have the anointing of God in your life, you are glad to notice that you are (super)naturally drawn to the things and people of God. If you stay home and say that you have the anointing, you are deceiving yourself. The anointing does not come cheaply, nor does it come in isolation. There is a price to pay for the anointing.

SEEKING THE ANOINTING AND ITS AUTHORITY

Do not sit and wait for the anointing to come to you. You must go and seek out the anointing. Many Christians today eschew stories of revival happening around the globe, across the border and down the road. They refuse to go and see for themselves, saying that if it is God's will, He will rain down His anointing upon them right where they stand. True, He can if He so chooses. However, the Scriptures record many examples of men and women of God paying a price to receive this most precious impartation.

Paul was blinded in an encounter with the Lord, but for him to get the anointing, he had to leave where he was and be led to Damascus, where he waited to receive what the Lord wanted him to have. For three days and three nights, Paul fasted. Only then did he received the anointing (see Acts 9:3-22). Did Paul rush out then and immediately begin his ministry to the Gentiles? No. Instead, God led him to Arabia and back to Damascus for three years of training in the anointing (see Gal. 1:15-21).

It is important to understand that having power in the anointing is not the same as having authority. Many receive the anointing and then declare that they are ready to take the world for God. As with Paul, however, we require training in how to walk in the authority of the Spirit. If you don't have the proper authority in the Spirit, you will abuse the power of God.

The anointing will open your eyes, but you need authority to operate in the anointing. Jesus Christ was full of the power of God, but He needed the anointing to open doors for Him. When He came out of the waters of the Jordan, the heavens opened and God declared, "This is My beloved Son, in whom I am well pleased" (Matt. 3:17). Later, God would again speak from heaven, saying, "This is My beloved Son, in whom I am well pleased. Hear Him!" (Matt. 17:5). Because of the anointing, people were inspired to hear the words of Jesus. But He began His ministry only after the Spirit had come upon Him.

If you want to begin a ministry, you need the anointing to open doors for you. If the anointing doesn't open doors for you, and you try to open doors with your own charisma or with the power of your words, you are going to get yourself into trouble. You need the anointing of God.

PATTERNS OF ANOINTING

In the natural, anointing means the act of pouring out oil as a sign of consecration for the work of God. When we anoint someone or something with oil, the oil is a symbol of His anointing. Spiritually speaking, oil is a symbol of the Holy Spirit. When the Holy Spirit comes upon us, he brings the true anointing of God. When you talk about the Holy Spirit, spiritually you are talking about the anointing. When you declare that the Spirit of God is upon you, you are saying that you have been anointed with the true presence of God.

In the Old Testament, any object to be used for God's work or for God's use had to first be anointed. Even raw materials were anointed. Genesis 31:13 speaks of pillars being anointed. Furnishings were anointed (see Exod. 30:26; Lev. 8:11). Today we have largely forgotten the pattern and value of anointing things for God's use. We might remember to anoint some special object with which God has blessed us, but the biblical pattern is to anoint *everything* for God's use.

How often do we get something new, like a new home or car, and in the excitement of the moment, forget to consecrate that item to God's use? I suggest to you that it is important to anoint a house or a car, especially if they have been used before and we have no idea of their history. Whatever a Christian puts his hand to becomes a reflection of God on this earth, and you need to set those things apart for God's use. Anything that is not set apart for His use is open to misuse.

WALKING IN THE ANOINTING IS NECESSARY IF WE ARE TO FULFILL GOD'S MANDATE FOR THE CHURCH.

In the Old Testament, when Solomon consecrated the Temple to God, they anointed the building for the invitation of God's presence. When I enter a new place where we are going to hold a meeting, whether it is a church auditorium or a hotel ballroom, I will spend time in prayer beforehand and consecrate that location to the Lord. I believe the anointing of God will remain on a place after we leave and bring conviction of sin to those who follow behind us. This includes hotel rooms or any place that we sleep. Anoint the places you go so that the presence of God might freely flow in that place while you are there and bring awareness of His presence after you leave.

I extend consecration to friendships. If you meet someone new and begin to grow close, your relationship needs to be given to God and anointed by Him. Take time to consecrate your relationships to God. You need anointed people around you.

In the Old Testament, people were also anointed to hold specific offices. Priests, prophets and kings all had to be anointed (see Exod. 28:41). According to the New Testament, we have all been redeemed by the blood of Christ to be kings and priests to our God (see Rev. 5:9,10). Priests are ones who go before the Lord, get the wisdom of the Lord and bring the wisdom to the people of God. They intercede and stand in the gap for the people. A king is one who knows what His people are to do. I believe that to be a good king is very similar to operating on the level of a prophet.

Every time God appointed a king in the Old Testament, a priest and a prophet were appointed to walk alongside that king. If we have been appointed kings and priests, we must become as prophets to express the full wisdom and counsel of God. I believe that is why the gifts of prophecy have been released in the Church. This level of anointing is necessary for us to fulfill His mandate for the Church.

SIGNS OF THE ANOINTING

When you have the anointing of the Lord upon you, there should be signs in evidence. Some people confuse the anointing with the gifts God has given His people. Many say they have the anointing, but all they really have is the gift of tongues. I speak in tongues, I believe in tongues and I appreciate the gift of tongues. But tongues do not take the place of the anointing. Tongues are given for prayer and for edification, but they are not the same as the anointing.

Anointing is not based on shouting or a level of excitement, although these at times may accompany the presence of the Holy Spirit. We have a tendency to gauge a minister's anointing by how loud he shouts, and some believe that if the preacher doesn't shout as loud as they think he should, he has missed the anointing! Many times, just the opposite is true. Those who shout the loudest can be those who most miss the mark, whether they are at the pulpit or among the congregation. You can occasionally find the biggest hypocrites and sinners shouting the loudest.

A word of instruction: It is very important when someone is ministering to you and the anointing is upon him or her that you receive the anointing rather than shouting back or praying or singing louder than the person ministering to you. If the anointing is operating, someone has to receive it. If you compete with the anointing at this point, there will be only spiritual conflict or confusion. Where the Spirit of the Lord resides, there is no confusion.

Whether it is in our preference for loud music or shouting to the Lord, many of us mistake volume or flash for the anointing. While there is nothing inherently wrong with enthusiastic worship, often it is only a product of the flesh. When Elijah was running from Jezebel and he needed to hear from the Lord, he heard and saw a mighty wind, an earthquake and fire, but the Lord was not in them. Instead, God spoke to his prophet in a still, small voice (see 1 Kings 19:11-13).

You can be in the presence of the anointing, and you will not have to say a word or make a sound. You can feel the tangible presence of God. At times, you might be singing when the anointing of God comes, and you suddenly feel the need to stop singing. God will do a quiet work. He will begin to put the spiritual mirror before you, and you will see yourself—what you used to be and what He has made of you. The anointing will hit you, and it will begin to break those things of the heart and mind that stand in the way of God's work. When the anointing begins to operate in your life, it causes you to yield and change. Remember, the true anointing is not just noise or outward manifestations but fruits that come from a solid tree. The anointing brings change.

Don't misunderstand me to say that the anointing never manifests in loud noises or powerful displays. That happens, too. I often make a lot of noise when the Spirit of God comes upon me, especially when the anointing manifests in fervent prayer. However, you must be sensitive to the moods of the Holy Spirit. His anointing reflects the moods of God. At times, He doesn't want to make any noise but, rather, to come in quietly and sit beside you. Other times, the Holy Spirit will come in quietly, but His anointing will shake you up and cause you to be revived and strengthened.

ARE YOU CONTAGIOUS?

When you have the anointing of God upon you, and you allow the anointing to flow freely in your life, you will become contagious, and anyone who comes close to you will somehow be affected by the anointing. Let me ask you this: How many people have been affected by the anointing that is upon your life?

I'm not asking how many people you have shouted to. The anointing affects. The anointing is contagious. The anointing should show forth in your life without you having to say much. People should feel the presence of God in your life.

You may say that you have chicken pox. But if you actually have the measles, measles are what you will transmit and what others will catch from you. You can only impart what you do have, and not what you do not have. So many Christians are confused about what they really have when it comes to the anointing. You cannot give to others what you don't have. You can try to convince yourself that you have something when you really don't. You can talk about it all you want, but the proof is in what you transfer to others. The anointing *will* show.

PURPOSES OF THE ANOINTING

People can have great ideas, even mighty and noble ideas. But, in truth, a little anointing is worth more than a thousand great ideas. If you have tremendous ideas and they are not anointed, you may as well put the those ideas on the shelf because they are not going to come to life. The reason we have so many dreamers today in our churches is because they have great ideas that are not anointed. If the ideas were anointed, they would bring forth great fruit.

God intends for all of us to be anointed by His Spirit. If the anointing is in your life, there will be no jealousy and no competition. Great ideas and ambition without the anointing are fruitless. The Bible calls this "chasing after the wind" (Eccles. 4:4, *NIV*). Many people are like that. Spurred on by envy, they labor over great plans but fail to pursue the anointing.

We need to pay attention to the anointing of God and allow it to form our ideas. We need to respect the anointing and not just take it for granted. It is better for you to stay at home on a Sunday and sleep in than it is to be in the presence of the anointing and not pay attention. It is dangerous for you to be where there is fire and afterwards walk about trailing smoke. People can choke on the smoke. You need to leave the presence of God with the fire of His anointing. Unless you are walking in the anointing, you are just smoke without fire.

I find it peculiar that many people think the anointing is found mainly on the pastor of a church. So people go around looking for the perfect church, a place where the pastor has the anointing, instead of seeking the anointing for themselves. Every believer in every congregation is to be a carrier of the anointing. Be open to the full anointing that God wants you to have!

Be careful, however, how you seek after the anointing. The anointing attracts those who seek it, but some people are always chasing the anointing from place to place, searching for someone new who carries a fresh anointing. Undue searching is a sign of immaturity, carnality and a lack of spiritual understanding. The same is true of people who will not go to church when their pastor is out of town. We need to understand that we are all carriers of the Holy Spirit, and the dynamic of the whole congregation is changed by our presence, whether or not the regular pastor is in the pulpit.

There are, of course, times when it is necessary and good to be inspired by the teaching of others, but don't run after the anointing in a dangerous fashion. You can know whether a person has genuine anointing by watching their lives. A genuinely anointed person is stable. If someone has charisma and they are not stable, do not follow them. Their anointing may, in fact, be a bewitching spirit, a merchandising spirit or a cheating spirit. I have seen too many people be impressed or tricked by false things that seem like the anointing. Allow the true anointing to mature you and make you discerning.

PRACTICAL USE OF THE ANOINTING

We need the anointing every moment of our lives. We need the anointing when we sleep. We need the anointing when we wake up. We need the anointing when we are brushing our teeth— everything every day of our lives. I believe one reason we are seeing so many problems in our society (and even in the Church) today is because of the absence of the anointing. The people are under greater bondage because people no longer have respect for the anointing of God.

But God wants to anoint us. The anointing is the answer, the antidote to society's ills:

> It shall come to pass in that day that his burden will be taken away from your shoulder, and his yoke from your neck, and the yoke will be destroyed because of the anointing oil (Isa. 10:27).

If you have Jesus Christ in you, you have the Anointed One. You can make a difference in this world. You can see bondages broken and circumstances changed all around you. Yokes which come upon you must be broken because of Christ.

The *New International Version* says that "in that day . . . the yoke will be broken because you have grown so fat" with the anointing of the Lord! Many Christians have grown so lean. They have the anointing, but they are not walking in the anointing. Most people love Jesus, but their lives are not very powerful in God. We need His anointing to break the yokes on our jobs, in our families, over our health. If your children are rebelling and you have lost control, you need the anointing to break this yoke and get your house in order. If things aren't going well in your marriage, that's a sign that you need the anointing. If you have no hunger for the Word or you have grown insensitive to the things of God, you need the anointing.

We need the anointing to be promoted in our jobs, to work well, to respect our bosses and to cooperate with our coworkers. If we do not respect the anointing, we will not prosper in these things. The anointing can break the yoke of those things that stand in your way, whether your problem is addiction, lying, stealing, rebellion, laziness or fear. When you have the anointing and are led by the Spirit, you will be in the right places at the right times.

When you have the anointing, no one has to tell you when to pray. Your life will be orderly. You will worship God in your actions and your giving. You will read your Bible. You will want to be in church, focused on the things of God. Your life will be different. You will have answers for your family and for your work. You will have direction.

The anointing will allow you to freely and boldly raise your hands and testify of the things of God, anywhere, anytime. Don't fool yourself into thinking you have the anointing of the Spirit of God if you are too embarrassed to show it! Don't tell me you have the anointing when you cannot raise your hands or pray with your wife or speak out about the things of God to someone else.

We desperately need the anointing of God. Most people come to church and say to the pastor, "Wonderful service!" on their way out the door, but their lives don't change. We need the anointing for change and to fulfill the call of God on our lives.

Otherwise, there's no need to waste your time sitting in the house of God.

When Jesus declared that the Spirit of God had come upon Him, He also declared the five things that the Spirit was commissioning Him to do (see Luke 4:18):

1. Preach the gospel to the poor.
2. Heal the brokenhearted.
3. Proclaim liberty to the captives and recovery of sight to the blind.
4. Set at liberty those who are oppressed.
5. Proclaim the acceptable year of the Lord.

These were not just things for Jesus to do; all Christians are meant to do these things in the Spirit of God. This is a far cry from simply attending a church! We are given the anointing of God for a purpose: to bring change in ourselves, in our homes, among our friends and at our jobs!

When you tell the Lord that you want the anointing, you are asking for something big. But the Lord has made a way that we might have that anointing of the Holy Spirit through Jesus Christ. But the Lord is not interested in giving the anointing to a wicked and lazy servant who will not invest the anointing in doing the things of God (see Matt. 25:24-28). If you want the anointing to come and abide with you, become a good and faithful servant who uses the wonderful gifts He has given you—and He will give you more! (see Matt. 25:29).

APPENDIX

For more information about the contributing authors or to contact their ministries, please call or write:

CHÉ AHN
Harvest Rock Church
Harvest International Ministries
1539 E. Howard Street
Pasadena, CA 91104
Phone: (626) 794-1199
Fax: (626) 797-7964
E-mail: harvestrk@aol.com
http://www.harvestrockchurch.org

JOHN ARNOTT
Toronto Airport Christian Fellowship
272 Attwell Drive
Toronto, ON M9W 6M3
Phone: (416) 674-8463
Fax: (416) 674-8465
E-mail: mail@tacf.org
http://www.tacf.org

FRANK DAMAZIO
City Bible Church
9200 NE Fremont
Portland, OR 97220-3610
Phone: (503) 255-2224
Fax: (503) 256-9637
E-mail: pastoral@citybiblechurch.org
http://www.citybiblechurch.org

LOU ENGLE
Harvest Rock Church
1539 E. Howard Street
Pasadena, CA 91104
Phone: (626) 794-1199
Fax: (626) 296-7605
E-mail: louengle@familyclick.com

KINGSLEY FLETCHER
Kingsley Fletcher Ministries
P.O. Box 12017
Research Triangle Park, NC 27709-2017
Phone: (919) 382-1944
Fax: (919) 382-3360
E-mail: kfm@kfmlife.org
http://www.kfmlife.org

CINDY JACOBS
Generals of Intercession
P.O. Box 49788
Colorado Springs, CO 80949
Phone: (719) 535-0977
Fax: (719) 535-0884
E-mail: genint@aol.com
http://www.generals.org

JOHN KILPATRICK
Brownsville Assembly of God
3100 W. DeSoto Street
Pensacola, FL 32505
Phone: (850) 433-3078
E-mail: ministry@brownsvilleag.org
http://www.brownsville-revival.org

BART PIERCE
1607 Cromwell Bridge Road
Baltimore, MD 21234
Phone: (410) 882-4967
E-mail: rcc@rockcitychurch.com
http://www.rockcitychurch.com

WINKIE PRATNEY
P.O. Box 876
Lindale, TX 75771
Phone: (903) 882-8501
E-mail: winkprat@aol.com
http://www.gospelcom.net/moh

SERGIO SCATAGLINI
Scataglini Ministries, Inc.
P.O. Box 2323
Elkhart, IN 46515-2323
Phone: (219) 389-7729
Fax: (219) 296-7729
E-mail: info@scataglini.com
http://www.scataglini.com

WENDELL SMITH
The City Church
9051 132nd Avenue NE
Kirkland, WA 98033
Phone: (425) 803-3233
Fax: (425) 889-8940
E-mail: info@thecity.org
http://www.thecity.org

Tommy Tenney

GodChasers.network
P.O. Box 3355
Pineville, LA 71361-3355
Phone: (318) 442-4273
Fax: (318) 442-6884
E-mail: info@godchasers.net
http://www.godchasers.net